WAR in the
PACIFIC

Richard OVERY
Foreword by Dale DYE

SEVENOAKS

★ CONTENTS

OPERATIONS MAP:
Japanese Expansion
1941–42 8

IMPERIAL JAPAN 10

PEARL HARBOR 12

BLITZKRIEG IN ASIA 14

CORREGIDOR:
Fall of the Philippines 16

OPERATIONS MAP 1942 18

THE BATTLE OF CORAL SEA 20

THE BATTLE OF MIDWAY 22

BATTLE FOR THE SOLOMONS 24

GUADALCANAL 26

OPERATIONS MAP 1943 28

OPERATION "CARTWHEEL":
War for New Guinea 30

ISLAND HOPPING IN THE PACIFIC:
Gilbert and Marshall Islands 32

OPERATIONS MAP 1944 34

THE MARIANAS:
Defence to the Death 36

BATTLE OF THE PHILIPPINE SEA 38

THE BATTLE OF PELELIU 40

THE RECAPTURE OF THE
PHILIPPINES 42

THE BATTLE OF LEYTE GULF 44

OPERATIONS MAP 1945 46

IWO JIMA 48

THE FIREBOMBING OF TOKYO 50

OKINAWA 52

THE ATOMIC BOMBS 54

THE JAPANESE SURRENDER 56

INDEX 58

ACKNOWLEDGEMENTS 60

Design and maps © Carlton Books Limited 2010, 2011
Text © Richard Overy 2010

This edition published in 2011 by SevenOaks
A division of the Carlton Publishing Group
20 Mortimer Street, London W1T 3JW

Printed in China
All rights reserved
A CIP catalogue for this book is available from the British Library
ISBN: 978 1 86200 859 5

FOREWORD

By Captain Dale A. Dye USMC (Ret.)

Spend time talking to our dwindling number of living World War II veterans and you'll likely notice a subtle difference between what you hear from those who served in Europe and those who fought in the Pacific. Combat, whether it was on the ground, in the air or at sea, is the common denominator and you'll cringe at similar tales of exhaustion, deprivation, brutality and fear. Probe a bit and you'll find bitterness among the veterans that faced the Japanese in fighting across the vast reaches of the Pacific that's often curiously absent in the memories of their brethren who slugged it out with German forces in the European Theater of Operations.

"Listen here," said one American Navy gunner's mate who survived the sinking of the USS *Vincennes* at the Battle of Savo Island during the Solomons Campaign in 1942, "we didn't even have a short-hand for where we were tangling with the Japs. You'd read about this or that happening in the ETO, but nobody gave a damn about us. We didn't even know where we were half the time. It was just somewhere in the South Pacific and anyplace out there was bad enough."

His comments reflect the attitude of many who fought the marauding Imperial Japanese Army in remote, unfamiliar and often unpronounceable locations in the vast stretches of the Pacific during World War II. Even after the infamous Japanese sneak attack on the U.S. Naval Base at Pearl Harbor in 1941 which emphasized the significant Japanese threat to the free world, they were a second priority to the Allies' primary concern of defeating Hitler's forces in Europe. And they faced a significantly different enemy in very different battle zones than what other Allied forces were dealing with in North Africa, the Mediterranean and on the European continent.

Battles are won by fire and maneuver. Wars are won by logistics and in the Pacific, the Allied logistical tail stretched precariously over thousands of miles of open ocean patrolled and controlled early in the war by a deadly combination of Japanese warships and carrier-based combat aircraft. Consider that after the D-Day invasion in 1944, the Allied forces grinding through German defenders in France only had to reach back across the narrow English Channel for resupply or reinforcement, a matter of days at most. In the Pacific, it was most often a matter of weeks or months before vital war materiel and manpower reached army and Marine forces fighting on remote islands and atolls. In the meantime, soldiers and Marines bleeding and dying on Guadalcanal, Bougainville, Guam, Saipan, Tarawa and Peleliu just had to make do with what they carried ashore or captured from the Japanese defenders. In the Pacific, getting ashore to engage the Japanese was often the easiest part of the most difficult of all combat maneuvers, the amphibious assault. The hard part – especially in the early Pacific campaigns of World War II – was staying ashore and surviving against fanatical Japanese defenders who refused to give an inch or surrender in the face of overwhelming firepower. The celebrated 1st Marine Division that carried out the first offensive move of the war against Japanese forces at Guadalcanal was stranded on that jungle island when the Navy task force that delivered them to the Solomons departed under threat of Japanese air and surface attacks taking much of the division's supply with them and leaving the Marines to hang on by their bloody fingernails.

It was often a similar story as Allied forces crawled slowly and painfully across the Pacific, sometimes responding to General Douglas MacArthur and sometimes to Admiral Chester Nimitz or other Allied commanders in a confusing division of territory and conflicting strategies. Along the way, they practiced and perfected amphibious tactics and combat techniques that served and succeeded on battlefields where – unlike infantry engagements in Europe – close combat was very often defined by the length of a bayonet. And when that bayonet was being shoved around by a Japanese soldier, schooled in the way of bushido, another significant difference between war in Europe and war in the Pacific became painfully obvious.

War with the Japanese in the Pacific – especially infantry combat on coral beaches or jungle forests – was brutal beyond imagination simply because the Japanese soldier thought and fought differently with a fanatical, no quarter psychology that differed shockingly from the Western approach to warfare. For the most part, defeating the Japanese required killing them, often in a manner so brutal and barbaric that it left livid scars in the minds of the Westerners doing the necessary work required to stem the Japanese tide of conquest in the Pacific.

With the exception of a few iconic images such as the flag-raising by U.S. Marines on Iwo Jima and MacArthur wading ashore in his return to the Philippines, World War II in the Pacific has been overshadowed by the more accessible and understandable campaigns in Europe. With this book and its marvelous, rare reproductions, we hope to shed some much-needed light on the service and sacrifice of the gallant men and women who served in the Pacific War.

INTRODUCTION

The war between the Japanese Empire and the United States and British Commonwealth in the Pacific Ocean area was the bloodiest and hardest fought of the campaigns waged by the Western Allies. Yet in many general accounts of the war the Pacific is given much less weight than the European theater and its strategic significance played down. The comprehensive defeat of Japan was nevertheless a vital component of Allied war aims and the Pacific was an arena of war that taxed Allied fighting power to the limit.

Japanese leaders assumed that once they had captured the Pacific region and neutralized the U.S. fleet at Pearl Harbor they could begin to remodel the whole area as the Japanese "New Order". They assumed that war across thousands of miles of ocean would be difficult for their enemies to conduct and that the Western powers lacked the will for a major contest. They hoped that some kind of agreement would recognize Japanese domination of Eastern Asia and the Pacific. In this they misjudged profoundly the determination of their enemies to halt aggression and destroy Japanese militarism. Little was to be expected of the war in Asia, where Japanese armies remained bogged down in a long war with Chinese Nationalists and Communists. The key to the defeat of Japan was the long war in the ocean fought predominantly by American naval and army forces, supported by Australian troops and ships and, late in the war, by the Royal Navy.

This present volume is designed to bring alive that Pacific conflict with the help of recorded memories, photographs, and reproductions of key documents and memorabilia. The campaign area was vast, covering thousands of miles of ocean. Unlike the European campaigns, most of the sites of fierce fighting were small islands with no industry, few towns, and tiny populations. The conditions of combat were harsh for both sides, with high temperatures, endemic diseases, hostile jungle terrain, and volcanic or coral surfaces. Little quarter was given or expected and remarkably few men were captured on either side compared with the high prisoner numbers in the European war. The exceptionally harsh conditions of combat brought out suicidal bravery on both sides. Many of the surviving legends of wartime heroism in both the United States and Japan come from the battles of the Pacific War. So fanatical was Japanese resistance in a society where surrender was profoundly dishonouring that in the end the defeat of Japan required the obliterating damage inflicted from May 1945 by the U.S. air forces. Two very different kinds of war, one on the ground, the other in the air, finally brought the brief era of Japan's "New Order" to an end.

Richard Overy

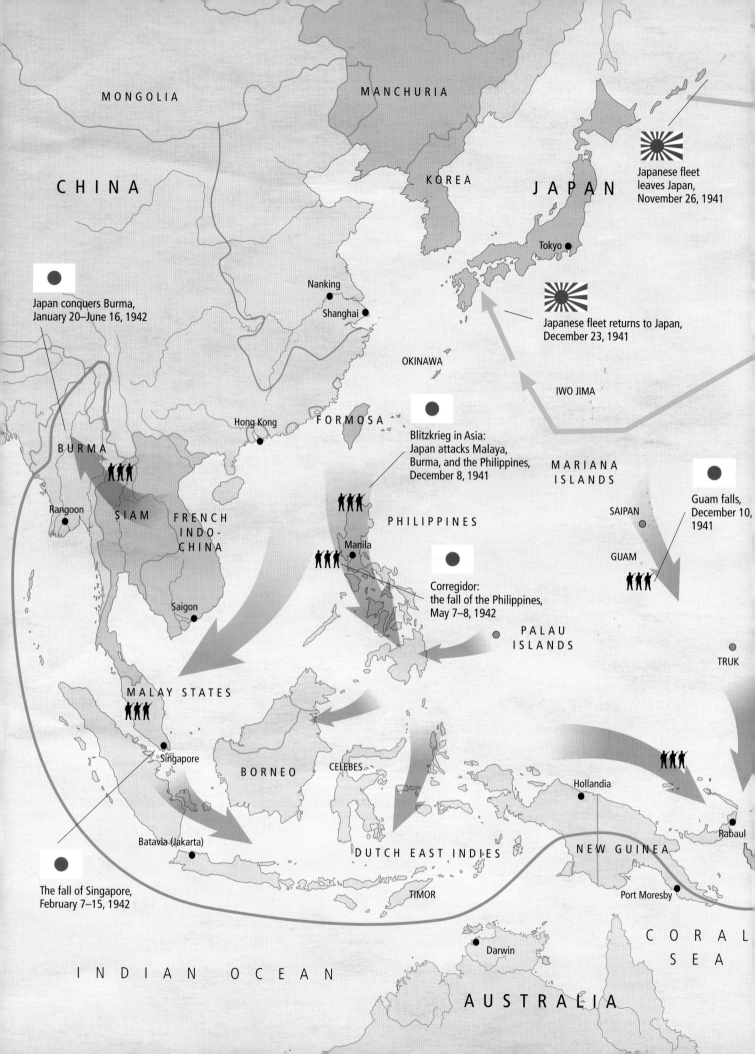

MONGOLIA

MANCHURIA

CHINA

KOREA

JAPAN

Japanese fleet
leaves Japan,
November 26, 1941

Tokyo

Nanking

Shanghai

Japanese fleet returns to Japan,
December 23, 1941

Japan conquers Burma,
January 20–June 16, 1942

OKINAWA

IWO JIMA

Hong Kong

FORMOSA

BURMA

Rangoon

SIAM

FRENCH
INDO-
CHINA

Blitzkrieg in Asia:
Japan attacks Malaya,
Burma, and the Philippines,
December 8, 1941

MARIANA
ISLANDS

PHILIPPINES

SAIPAN

Guam falls,
December 10,
1941

Manila

GUAM

Saigon

Corregidor:
the fall of the Philippines,
May 7–8, 1942

PALAU
ISLANDS

TRUK

MALAY STATES

Singapore

BORNEO

CELEBES

Hollandia

NEW GUINEA

Rabaul

Batavia (Jakarta)

DUTCH EAST INDIES

The fall of Singapore,
February 7–15, 1942

TIMOR

Port Moresby

Darwin

CORAL
SEA

INDIAN OCEAN

AUSTRALIA

JAPANESE EXPANSION 1941-42

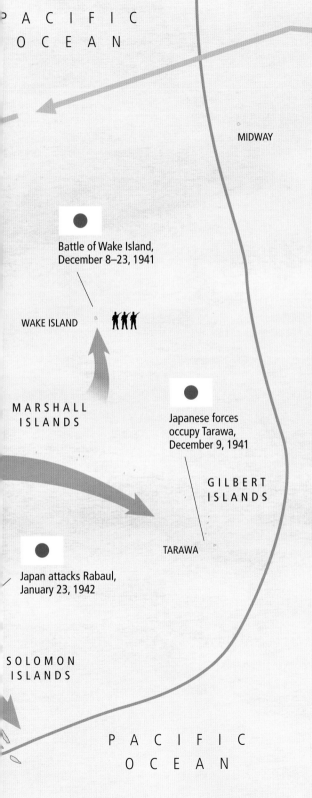

PACIFIC OCEAN

MIDWAY

Battle of Wake Island,
December 8–23, 1941

WAKE ISLAND

MARSHALL
ISLANDS

Japanese forces
occupy Tarawa,
December 9, 1941

GILBERT
ISLANDS

TARAWA

Japan attacks Rabaul,
January 23, 1942

SOLOMON
ISLANDS

PACIFIC
OCEAN

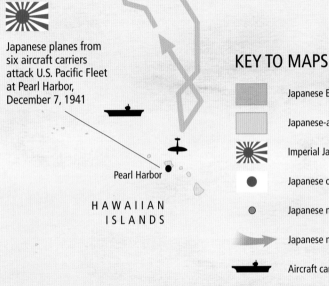

Japanese planes from
six aircraft carriers
attack U.S. Pacific Fleet
at Pearl Harbor,
December 7, 1941

Pearl Harbor

HAWAIIAN
ISLANDS

KEY TO MAPS

	Japanese Empire 1942
	Japanese-allied states
	Imperial Japanese Navy
	Japanese occupations
	Japanese military bases
	Japanese military advances
	Aircraft carrier fleet
	Army land battles
	Air attacks
	Limit of Japanese expansion

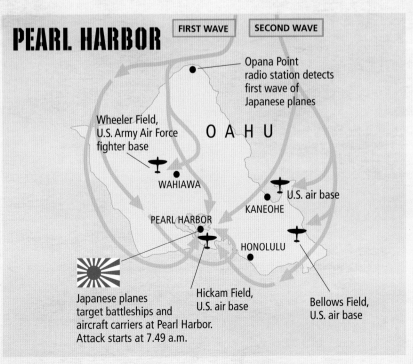

PEARL HARBOR

FIRST WAVE   **SECOND WAVE**

Opana Point
radio station detects
first wave of
Japanese planes

Wheeler Field,
U.S. Army Air Force
fighter base

OAHU

WAHIAWA

U.S. air base

KANEOHE

PEARL HARBOR

HONOLULU

Japanese planes
target battleships and
aircraft carriers at Pearl Harbor.
Attack starts at 7.49 a.m.

Hickam Field,
U.S. air base

Bellows Field,
U.S. air base

IMPERIAL JAPAN

ABOVE The military cap of a Superior Private in the Japanese Imperial Army.

LEFT Chiang Kaishek, the leader of the nationalist Guomindang, ruled two-thirds of the country by 1936. By 1939 this united China had been shattered.

Japan had been an imperial power since the nineteenth century, annexing present-day Taiwan in 1895 and Korea in 1910. In May 1915, Japan began to encroach on Chinese sovereignty as China collapsed into political chaos, its territory fought over by competing warlords. In the 1920s a Japanese army – the Kwantung – was stationed in the northern Chinese province of Manchuria to safeguard Japanese economic interests. The military leadership was keen to increase Japan's imperial influence in China, and the rise of Chinese nationalism – directed at the Japanese presence – and the catastrophic effects of the 1929 world slump on Japan's economic prospects were used as excuses for the Japanese army, largely independent of the government in Tokyo, to embark on a programme of military expansion in Asia.

In September 1931, the Kwantung Army staged a clumsy fake attack on a Japanese-controlled railway near Mukden in Manchuria, and the incident was then used to justify the rapid Japanese occupation of much of the province and Manchuria's rich mineral and food supplies were brought under Japanese control. Although a member of the League, Japan's aggression was not reversed by the other powers, and in 1933 Japan left the organization. Over the next three years, Japan's army pushed down into northern China, taking control of the provinces of Jehol, Chahar and Hopeh, and stationing a garrison in the old imperial capital of Beijing.

Growing Chinese resistance sucked the Japanese army into further aggression: a small incident at the Marco Polo Bridge near Beijing on July 7 rapidly escalated. On July 27, the Japanese prime minister, Prince Konoye, declared that Japan was now going to create a "New Order" in Asia. Within weeks, a full-scale war began between Chinese Nationalist and Communist forces and the Japanese army of occupation, which ended only with Japan's surrender eight years later.

ABOVE Two Japanese soldiers stand guard on top of a train in Manchuria in December 1931 to warn of the approach of Chinese bandit forces following the seizure of the province in September that year.

RIGHT Communist leaders Mao Zedong and Zhou Enlai during the Long March of Chinese Communists in 1934 to the Chinese interior province of Yan'an. Around 100,000 trekked the 5,000 miles (8,000 kilometers) to escape Chinese Nationalists.

THE "RAPE OF NANKING"

On December 13, 1937, the Japanese army captured Chiang Kaishek's capital at Nanjing. What followed was one of the most horrific episodes in the long Sino-Japanese conflict. Japanese forces were allowed weeks of uninhibited violence against the defenceless population while their commander, General Iwane Matsui, proved powerless to stop them. Post-war estimates suggest that between 260,000 and 350,000 Chinese were murdered, most of them amid scenes of terrible cruelty. All 90,000 Chinese soldiers taken prisoner were killed, some in beheading competitions. Tens of thousands of Chinese women of all ages were raped and then killed. The Japanese army, Matsui told an American journalist a few days later, was "probably the most undisciplined army in the world".

RIGHT Japanese soldiers using stripped and bound Chinese men as live targets for bayonet practice after the capture of the Chinese capital in December 1937.

Using the railways and river valleys, Japanese forces spread rapidly into central China, capturing Shanghai in October 1937, the Chinese Nationalist capital Nanjing in December. By 1939, Japan dominated most of the major cities and arteries of communication, from the southern Yangtze River to the northern province of Inner Mongolia.

The sudden expansion of Japanese imperial power destroyed the unified Chinese state Chiang Kaishek had tried to create. It brought Japan into conflict with the Western powers, which tolerated Japanese aggression only because there was no effective way of expelling Japan's army except at the cost of a major war that they had neither the will nor resources to engage in. When Japanese expansion did pose a direct threat to Soviet interests in Mongolia, two short campaigns resulted, at Changkufen in 1938 and at Nomonhan in 1939, both won by the Soviet Red Army. Japan's government and armed forces preferred to look south to the rich oilfields and minerals of the old European empires for the next stage of the construction of the Asian New Order.

In July 1940, when the first Japanese forces entered northern Indo-China, Roosevelt authorized restrictions of scrap steel and oil exports to Japan. Japanese naval planners, anxious about the threat of a total oil embargo, began to argue in favour of a pre-emptive "Southward Advance" against America and the British Empire, seizing the oil-rich region of the Dutch East Indies and establishing an unassailable perimeter in the Pacific.

The German invasion of the Soviet Union created confusion in Japan. The powerful Japanese army argued for the opportunity to settle accounts with Russia by joining forces with Germany in the destruction of the Soviet Union. The navy continued to press for a southern strategy on the grounds that the Soviet-German war reduced any risk in the north, while seizing the rich resources of the south would create conditions for the final triumph against China and the Soviet Union. On July 26, 1941, following further Japanese incursion in Indo-China, the United States froze all Japanese assets and tightened the oil embargo. The navy in early September 1941 proposed a showdown with the United States if diplomatic efforts to reverse American policy were not successful. A deadline was set for November 30, after which war would be launched. The American government could read Japanese codes and knew that Japanese plans for aggression were hardening. On November 26, Cordell Hull, Roosevelt's Secretary of State, presented new conditions to Japan for the withdrawal of their forces from Indo-China and China. The Japanese government rejected the idea out of hand, and on December 1, Emperor Hirohito approved the onset of war.

THE TRIPARTITE PACT

In November 1936 Japan first aligned itself with Nazi Germany when it signed the Anti-Comintern Pact. They shared not only a common hostility to communism but also a mutual commitment to revising the existing international system in their favour. In June 1940, joined by Italy, Germany and Japan negotiated what would become the Tripartite Pact. Signed in Berlin on September 27, 1940, it confirmed that Europe was the sphere for a New Order created by Germany and Italy, while Japan was free to construct a New Order in eastern Asia. All three pledged to come to the aid of the others if they were attacked by a third party not already at war. This clause was a warning to the U.S. and Japan hoped to be able to use the Pact as a bargaining counter with America, but it only served to confirm the view that the three states were intent on a dangerous transformation of the world order.

BELOW The destruction of the railway station in Shanghai during the Japanese attack in 1937. The Japanese used bombing indiscriminately in China, including poison gas.

INSET BELOW Japanese forces advance through the Indo-Chinese port of Haiphong, November 24, 1940. The Vichy French authorities were forced to accept the stationing of Japanese troops in the French colony along the Yunnan–Haiphong railway which had been used to supply Chinese forces in their war with Japan.

HAIPHONG

PEARL HARBOR

GENERAL HIDEKI TOJO (1884–1948)

General Tojo, the son of a Japanese army general, was appointed Army Minister in 1940 and then Prime Minister on 16 October 1941. He had little campaign experience, but was a hard-working, strict and effective administrator and military politician. He was a committed nationalist and was at the forefront of those arguing for a tough military policy in China and against compromise with the Western powers. He faced growing criticism in 1944 over Japanese military reverses and was forced to resign in July 1944. He tried and failed to commit suicide when American military police arrived to arrest him in 1945, and was hanged as a war criminal in December 1948.

The opening battle of Japan's Pacific campaign was a remarkably one-sided one. Once the decision for war had been taken, the plan for an assault on the U.S. naval base at Pearl Harbor in Hawaii was given the go-ahead. Japanese leaders hoped that the U.S. Pacific Fleet would be so heavily damaged that it would take valuable time before the American Navy could intervene against Japanese operations. In the meantime, Japan would have carved out its new Pacific area and reinforced its wide perimeter.

Preparations in Hawaii to meet a Japanese threat proved far from adequate. Little thought had been given to a possible aircraft carrier attack and the naval commander, Rear Admiral Husband E. Kimmel, assumed that any Japanese move would be made from the Marshall Islands far to the southwest, probably in the form of sabotage or spoiling attacks by submarines. U.S. intelligence also believed that the Philippines was a more likely target for attack, and many of the fighter aircraft stationed in Hawaii were moved to Wake and Midway Islands to help protect B-17 bombers being ferried out to air bases in the Philippines. Intelligence had intercepted Japanese instructions to spies in Hawaii to provide detailed information about Pearl Harbor but did not pass this on to Kimmel. The U.S. Army commander in Hawaii, Lieutenant General Walter Short, was also told to expect sabotage but no direct attack and no emergency provision was made for any attack of a more serious nature. Even if the Japanese decision to begin war against the United States had been discovered from intercepted diplomatic traffic, it is unlikely that Hawaii would have been regarded as a particularly vulnerable target.

By November 18 the Japanese task force of six Japanese aircraft carriers and supporting naval vessels, under the command of Vice-Admiral Chuichi Nagumo, had sailed from the Kurile Islands towards the north of Hawaii. They kept complete radio silence and remained invisible to the defenders at Pearl Harbor. They arrived 275 miles (442 kilometers) north of the naval base during the night of December 6/7 and prepared for an assault to be launched at 6 a.m. by naval aircraft. The only U.S. reconnaissance planes in the air on the day the attack began were far to the southwest, patrolling the area towards the Marshall Islands. U.S. radar picked up evidence of incoming aircraft but the inexperienced operators were told it was a force of B-17 bombers.

ABOVE LEFT A Japanese navy Mitsubishi "Zero" fighter takes off from the flight-deck of the Japanese carrier *Akagi* on the way to attack the U.S. naval base at Pearl Harbor on the morning of December 7, 1941. The Japanese navy had a corps of around 600 elite pilots who trained for long over-sea flights prior to the attack.

LEFT Purple heart awarded posthumously to Private Jack H. Feldman who died in the Japanese attack on Pearl Harbor at the age of only 19.

BELOW A Japanese aerial photograph of Ford Island in the Hawaii group after the Japanese attack on December 7, 1941. Two aircraft are visible pressing home further attacks on the U.S. fleet.

ABOVE U.S. President Franklin D. Roosevelt signs the document declaring war on Japan, December 8, 1941.

JAPANESE-AMERICANS

In 1942 around 110,000 Japanese-Americans, many of them American citizens, were "relocated" from their homes, mainly on the West Coast, to ten camps further inland. The move followed President Roosevelt's Executive Order 9066, signed on February 19, 1942, which gave the Secretary of War the right to designate prescribed military areas from which people could be legally and forcibly expelled. Most of the Japanese-Americans were held in the camps for up to three years even though not a single case of spying or sabotage was ever discovered. The same rules were not applied to American citizens of German or Italian descent, but only to German and Italian aliens. Around 22,500 young Japanese-American men volunteered for combat, 18,000 of whom served in segregated units.

BELOW USS *Shaw* explodes during the Japanese attack on Pearl Harbor. She was hit three times during the Japanese bombardment. She was not ready for action again until June 1942.

ABOVE Blazing oil from fractured fuel tanks in the aftermath of the Japanese bombing of the port installations at Pearl Harbor. A damaged battleship is visible behind the screen of smoke.

BELOW A naval launch approaches the U.S. battleship *West Virginia*, hit by six torpedoes during the attack by Japanese aircraft on the base at Pearl Harbor. Altogether 2,403 civilians and servicemen were killed in the attacks.

The Japanese plan was to send two waves of aircraft, piloted by highly-trained naval officers, to attack the naval base and nearby airfields, supported by a fleet of submarines that would finish off any surviving American ships. One of the midget submarines was sunk by a U.S. destroyer at 6.45 that morning, but there was no alert given to the island to expect an attack. When the first wave of 183 Japanese bombers, torpedo bombers, dive bombers and fighters struck at 7.49 a.m. on December 7 they achieved complete surprise.

A second wave followed at 8.50 a.m. with high-level bomb attacks, followed by renewed dive-bombing. The whole operation was over by 9.45 a.m. The impact was devastating, though the strategic consequences proved less profound than Japanese planners had hoped. Of the 394 U.S. aircraft on the island, 347 were destroyed or damaged for the loss of only 29 Japanese planes. In all 18 ships were sunk or damaged, including 8 battleships, and 2,403 servicemen and civilians were killed. But U.S. submarines were undamaged and by chance the aircraft carriers were at sea. Some 76 other vessels remained undamaged. Nagumo, wrongly fearful of a possible counter-attack, cancelled a projected third wave of attack, which might have crippled the port facilities. The submarine fleet achieved nothing of what had been expected.

In Congress the following day President Roosevelt condemned "a date that will live in infamy" and war was formally declared against the Japanese Empire. Japanese politicians had hoped that the attack on Pearl Harbor would demoralize American opinion and limit the American war effort. As it turned out nothing could have prompted greater outrage and a stronger American urge to fight the war with Japan to the finish.

BLITZKRIEG IN ASIA

The Japanese attack on Pearl Harbor was planned to coincide with a number of complex and daring combined operations to seize Southeast Asia, the East Indies and a string of small islands in the western Pacific to secure supplies of oil, rubber, tin and other minerals, and to discourage the British and American governments from attempting the difficult and expensive task of recapturing the new southern zone of the Japanese Empire. Within four months the vast area of the European powers' empires in the Far East was under Japanese rule.

On December 7, a Japanese seaborne striking force under General Tomoyuki Yamashita assembled in the Gulf of Siam, destined the following day to occupy the Kra Isthmus in southern Thailand and to assault the British airfields in northern Malaya. Other strike forces prepared to seize Hong Kong, assault the Philippines, and then conquer the British and Dutch possessions in the East Indies. The campaign was an extraordinary success. In Malaya Yamashita commanded around 60,000 men, but defeated a British Empire force more than twice as large. The attempt by the Allied army to hold up the Japanese advance was half-hearted at best. By January 9, the Japanese were almost at the Malayan capital of Kuala Lumpur. Adept at jungle warfare and tactics of infiltration, the Japanese army proved an irresistible force against a poorly prepared enemy with limited air power. By January 31, Malaya had been abandoned and the British forces were withdrawn to the island of Singapore.

Japanese progress in the Philippines was less spectacular. The northernmost island of Batan was occupied on December 8 and the main island of Luzon assaulted by seaborne forces two days later. Further out in the Pacific, small islands were seized to prevent any threat from the central ocean area. The U.S. base at Guam was occupied on December 10.

ABOVE Japanese forces were among the first to master effective combined operations. Here Japanese soldiers haul an artillery piece onto the shore from the landing boats during one of many similar operations in the early weeks of 1942.

TOP RIGHT Badge of the 11th Indian Infantry Division, which eventually surrendered to the Japanese when Singapore fell on February 15, 1942.

GENERAL DOUGLAS MACARTHUR (1880–1964)

MacArthur was born into an upper-class American family, the son of a soldier. He was an outstanding officer cadet, scoring the highest marks ever achieved at the military academy at West Point. At the end of the First World War, he was already a brigadier general. In 1930, he served as Army Chief of Staff, and in 1935 went as military adviser to the Philippines, where he retired from the American army to become a Philippines field marshal. In July 1941, Roosevelt made him commander of U.S. forces in the Far East, and he organized the defence of the Philippines against Japanese assault. He was appointed Commander-in-Chief South West Pacific Area in April 1942, and despite his reputation for flamboyance and self-promotion, became an inspirational leader of men. After recapturing the Philippines in 1945, he was made commander-in-chief of all U.S. army forces in the Pacific. He became Supreme Commander Allied Powers in the post-war administration of Japan and played a key part in Japan's democratic reconstruction. He was finally relieved of command in April 1951 following arguments with President Truman over policy on the Korean War.

ABOVE Burning oil stocks after a Japanese air attack on Dutch bases in the Dutch East Indies during the three-month campaign for the archipelago. The oil of the region was one of the chief factors encouraging the Japanese attack.

BELOW Japanese soldiers of General Yamashita's force storm a British-held village during the rapid conquest of Malaya. In seven weeks a larger British Empire and Commonwealth force was relentlessly driven back by an army whose soldiers were regarded in the West as racially inferior.

ADMIRAL CHUICHI NAGUMO (1887–1944)

The leader of the operation at Pearl Harbor, Nagumo was regarded as a particularly aggressive and effective fleet commander, with a reputation for speaking his mind. He rose to prominence in the 1930s as a torpedo expert, and was among the circle of senior Japanese naval officers who favoured a confrontation with the United States. He followed up the Pearl Harbor attack with command of the raids on northern Australia, India and Ceylon (Sri Lanka) and at the Battle of Midway. The disaster at Midway showed the limits of his grasp of naval air power, and he was relieved of command, posted back to Japan and then, in 1944, to the Marianas. He committed suicide in July 1944 during the American invasion of Saipan.

ABOVE LEFT British prisoners being marched into captivity in the British colony of Hong Kong following a brief resistance in December 1941. Thousands of British and Empire prisoners perished in Japanese camps and labour service during the war.

The garrison on Wake Island resisted the first Japanese attack on December 11, but succumbed to a larger air and sea assault 12 days later. The attack on the East Indies, defended by Dutch, British, Australian and colonial troops, began a week later on December 15 with landings on the island of Borneo. In a daring series of combined operations the Japanese army swarmed out over the archipelago, targeting airfields and oil installations. One branch of the assault moved southeast to capture the British Solomon Islands. Admiral Takahashi's task force concentrated on driving through the central zone, taking Bali on February 19 and Timor the next day. The capital of the Dutch East Indies, Batavia (Jakarta), was captured on March 5. Japanese warships and aircraft hunted down surviving Allied shipping and destroyed it, although some of the Allied force was evacuated to Australia from Java, harried by Japanese aircraft. On February 19, to drive home the Japanese success, bomber aircraft destroyed a large part of the northern Australian port of Darwin. The Dutch surrendered on March 9, the rest of the Allies three days later.

Japanese plans worked almost like clockwork. There was no intention of creating a larger campaign area than their limited forces could protect and Australia was safe for the present. In the Indian Ocean the British naval presence, weakened by the sinking of HMS *Prince of Wales* and HMS *Repulse* on December 10, was challenged by a daring raid led by Vice Admiral Nagumo, whose task force attacked Colombo in Ceylon on April 5, 1942, then the naval base at Trincomalee, sinking four warships, including the carrier *Hermes*, the first to be sunk by carrier aircraft. There was no intention yet of extending the Japanese Empire into the Indian Ocean area, the aim being simply to undermine the delicate British political position in southern Asia and to warn Britain to stay at arm's length from the new Japanese Empire which had been established across thousands of miles in the space of little more than four months.

ABOVE CENTRE The aftermath of the Japanese air raid on the northern Australian port of Darwin on February 19, 1942. The raid, carried out by 242 bombers and fighters, mostly carrier-borne, was designed to disrupt Allied communications, and killed over 200 Australians.

BELOW On April 18, 1942 U.S. naval and air forces launched a reprisal raid on Tokyo and other Japanese cities with 16 B-25 bombers launched from the U.S. carrier *Hornet*. The bombers, seen here leaving the carrier, inflicted little physical damage but gave the American public a psychological boost.

CORREGIDOR: FALL OF THE PHILIPPINES

The only major United States presence in the western Pacific was in the Philippines, an island group south of Formosa (Taiwan) which had been taken over by the United States after the Spanish-American war of 1898, but which by 1941 enjoyed a semi-autonomous status under American supervision. The island group lay directly in the path of the Japanese assault on the oil and raw-material riches of Malaya and the East Indies. The Japanese planned to capture it within 50 days of the sustained air attacks on December 8 which signaled the start of their campaign. The forces opposed to the Japanese 14th Army under Lieutenant General Homma were a mixture of recently arrived American soldiers, some 30,000 strong, and five divisions of the poorly resourced Filipino army, numbering 110,000 men. The garrisons were scattered around the many islands of the archipelago, with the largest concentration on the island of Luzon. General MacArthur, the senior U.S. commander, had tried to strengthen the air component of the Philippines defence, including the addition of 35 of the new B-17 "Flying Fortress" bombers, but the reinforcement of the region was not a high priority in Washington.

The surprise Japanese attack on December 8 was made from air bases in Formosa by specially trained pilots in aircraft modified to cope with the long cross-sea flight. The U.S. aircraft on Luzon were almost all on the ground and undispersed. Half were destroyed in the first wave of attack, and more in the next two days. The battle for the Philippines was waged on the Allied side with no effective air power.

ABOVE Manuel Quezon was the first elected president of the independent Commonwealth of the Philippines in 1935. He left the islands with MacArthur in March 1942, and led the Philippines government-in-exile in Washington, where he died in 1944.

LEFT The besieged garrison in the fortress of Corregidor in the Malinta Tunnel. The room here houses the Signal Corps and the Finance Office. The fortress eventually held 11,000 men, who were forced to surrender on May 6.

LEFT Badge of the U.S. Philippines Division.

ABOVE Japanese soldiers assault an American-held pillbox with flame-throwers in the bitter fighting in May 1942 on the Bataan peninsula on Luzon, largest of the Philippine islands.

GENERAL MASAHARU HOMMA (1888-1946)

A successful career officer, Lieutenant General Homma had more understanding of the West than most Japanese commanders. He was a military attaché in London for a total of eight years and was briefly attached to British forces on the Western Front in 1918. He participated in the Japanese-Chinese war as a major general, and, despite his outspoken fears of the risks run by Japan, was chosen to command the Japanese 14th Army for the invasion of the Philippines. By May, the conquest was complete but the long delay in clearing the islands and Homma's liberal reputation disappointed the army leadership in Tokyo and he held no further operational commands for the remainder of the war. He was tried and executed in 1946 for the many atrocities committed by the troops under his command.

ABOVE A group of soldiers from the Filipino army surrender to the Japanese during the assault on the Philippines in the first months of 1942. The Filipino army comprised only a few divisions and although it fought back against the Japanese invaders alongside the American garrison, it was an unequal struggle.

GENERAL JONATHAN WAINWRIGHT (1883–1953)

Trained as a cavalryman, Lieutenant General Wainwright served in the First World War and in the interwar years commanded cavalry units during the period of their transition to armoured warfare. In September 1940, he was made a major general and sent to command the Philippines Division, which he led at the start of the Japanese invasion. He was promoted to head the 1st Philippine Corps before being made overall commander-in-chief of forces in the Philippines after General MacArthur had left for Australia on March 11, 1942. He surrendered after the final struggle for the fortress of Corregidor and was imprisoned in Manchukuo, the Japanese puppet-state in Manchuria, where he was liberated by the Red Army in August 1945. He returned to a ticker-tape welcome in New York on September 13, 1945.

ABOVE U.S. troops surrender to the Japanese army on the Bataan peninsula in April 1942. Around 78,000 American and Filipino soldiers went into captivity, where thousands died from overwork, disease and violent mistreatment.

Japanese air superiority also compelled the commander of the U.S. Asiatic Fleet, Admiral Thomas Hart, to withdraw U.S. naval shipping from the defence of Luzon. Small units of Japanese troops were landed over the following week, including a force on Mindanao, the main southern island in the group, where the air base at Davao was captured. On December 22, the main body of Homma's force landed on either side of Luzon island in an attempt to encircle the enemy's forces around the capital, Manila. Bowing to reality, MacArthur ordered his forces to retreat to the Bataan peninsula on the southern flank of Manila Bay, and moved his headquarters to the island fortress of Corregidor at the seaward end of Bataan.

Although they were short of military supplies and food, the army units on Bataan greatly outnumbered Homma's force – which had totaled 43,000 at the start of the campaign – and they held up the conquest of the island for almost three months. High Japanese casualties and the withdrawal of a division to help in the conquest of the Netherlands East Indies forced Homma to halt and wear down the Filipino and American defenders by siege. By March, when MacArthur was ordered to leave the Philippines, it was evident to the defenders that there would be no aid or reinforcement. Lieutenant General Wainwright, who was given overall command by MacArthur following

his own withdrawal to the safety of Australia, kept up a spirited defence, but when Homma attacked with fresh troops on April 3 the front collapsed, and on April 9 Major General Edward King, commanding the forces on Bataan, surrendered. Some 78,000 Filipino and American soldiers and civilians were taken captive and forced to walk 65 miles (100 kilometers) across the peninsula. The Bataan Death March, as it came to be known, saw atrocities routinely committed against prisoners already debilitated by hunger and disease.

Around 2,000 soldiers had escaped to join the garrison in Corregidor and here Wainwright made his last stand with a total of 11,000 men. The system of deep tunnels under the fortress housed extensive stores and offered protection to the defenders. But relentless Japanese aerial and artillery bombardment destroyed almost everything on the surface, including most of the heavy guns, and on May 5 Homma's 4th Division landed on the fortress island itself. On May 6, Wainwright surrendered to avoid further losses, and the following day announced the surrender of all forces throughout the Philippines. Fighting nonetheless continued as Japanese forces occupied all the outer islands. Some Filipinos escaped into the mountains to become guerrilla fighters. Forces on Negros only surrendered on June 3 and on Samar by June 9, bringing the conquest of the islands to an end. By this time, almost the whole southern region was in Japanese hands.

RIGHT A Filipino guerrilla fighter, Amicedo Farola, June 1944. Some Filipino soldiers retreated to the mountains in 1942 where they kept up a limited resistance against the Japanese occupiers as members of the People's Anti-Japanese Army.

LEFT Japanese soldiers celebrate their victory against a numerically larger force on the Bataan peninsula. The long samurai sword was a standard piece of Japanese army equipment.

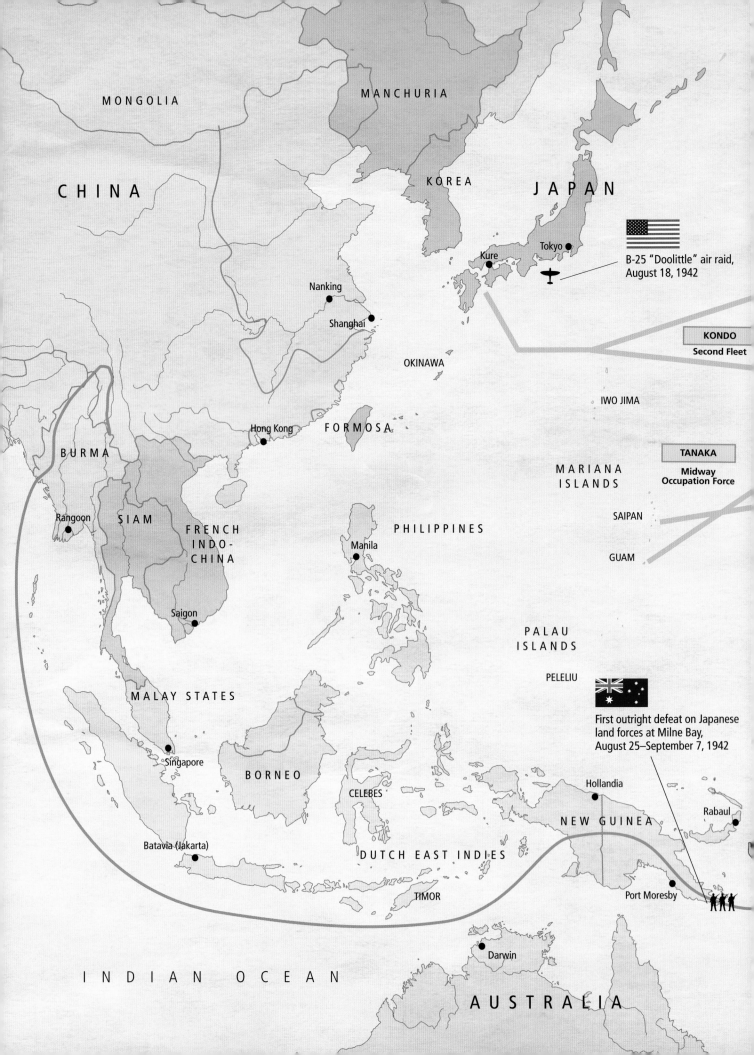

MONGOLIA

MANCHURIA

CHINA

KOREA

JAPAN

Nanking

Shanghai

Kure

Tokyo

B-25 "Doolittle" air raid, August 18, 1942

OKINAWA

KONDO
Second Fleet

IWO JIMA

BURMA

Hong Kong

FORMOSA

MARIANA ISLANDS

TANAKA
Midway Occupation Force

SAIPAN

Rangoon

SIAM

FRENCH INDO-CHINA

PHILIPPINES

Manila

GUAM

Saigon

PALAU ISLANDS

PELELIU

MALAY STATES

First outright defeat on Japanese land forces at Milne Bay, August 25–September 7, 1942

Singapore

BORNEO

Hollandia

Rabaul

CELEBES

NEW GUINEA

Batavia (Jakarta)

DUTCH EAST INDIES

Port Moresby

TIMOR

Darwin

INDIAN OCEAN

AUSTRALIA

PACIFIC THEATRE 1942

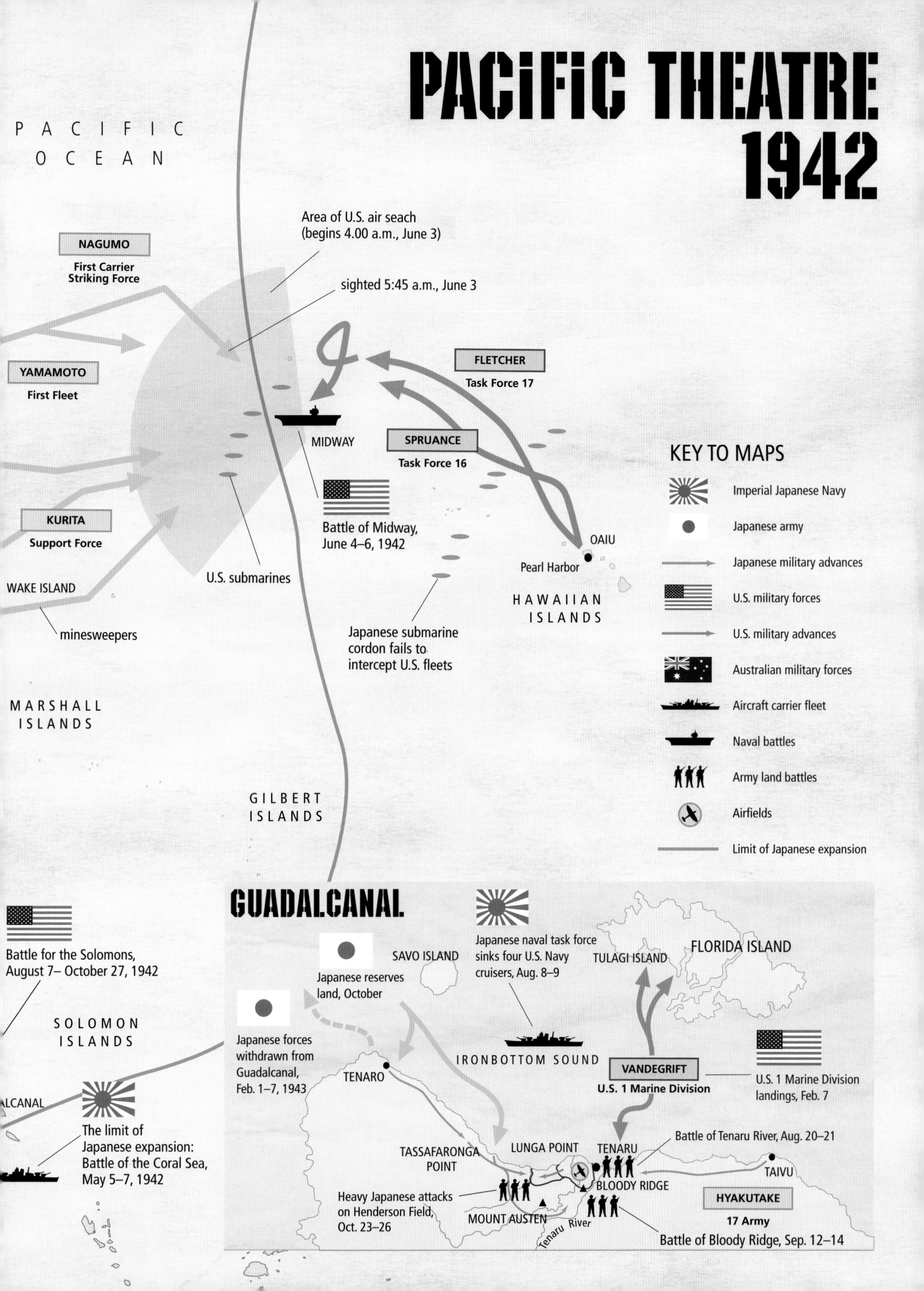

PACIFIC OCEAN

NAGUMO
First Carrier Striking Force

YAMAMOTO
First Fleet

KURITA
Support Force

WAKE ISLAND

minesweepers

MARSHALL ISLANDS

Area of U.S. air seach (begins 4.00 a.m., June 3)

sighted 5:45 a.m., June 3

MIDWAY

U.S. submarines

FLETCHER
Task Force 17

SPRUANCE
Task Force 16

Battle of Midway, June 4–6, 1942

Japanese submarine cordon fails to intercept U.S. fleets

OAIU

Pearl Harbor

HAWAIIAN ISLANDS

GILBERT ISLANDS

KEY TO MAPS

Imperial Japanese Navy

Japanese army

Japanese military advances

U.S. military forces

U.S. military advances

Australian military forces

Aircraft carrier fleet

Naval battles

Army land battles

Airfields

Limit of Japanese expansion

Battle for the Solomons, August 7– October 27, 1942

SOLOMON ISLANDS

ALCANAL

The limit of Japanese expansion: Battle of the Coral Sea, May 5–7, 1942

GUADALCANAL

Japanese reserves land, October

SAVO ISLAND

Japanese naval task force sinks four U.S. Navy cruisers, Aug. 8–9

FLORIDA ISLAND

TULAGI ISLAND

Japanese forces withdrawn from Guadalcanal, Feb. 1–7, 1943

TENARO

IRONBOTTOM SOUND

VANDEGRIFT
U.S. 1 Marine Division

U.S. 1 Marine Division landings, Feb. 7

TASSAFARONGA POINT

LUNGA POINT

TENARU

Battle of Tenaru River, Aug. 20–21

TAIVU

BLOODY RIDGE

HYAKUTAKE
17 Army

Heavy Japanese attacks on Henderson Field, Oct. 23–26

MOUNT AUSTEN

Tenaru River

Battle of Bloody Ridge, Sep. 12–14

THE BATTLE OF CORAL SEA

By early May 1942, Japan had almost accomplished the seizure of the southern region which had been planned for in 1941. The outer perimeter of the new imperial area was to be completed by the capture of the remaining southern part of the island of New Guinea, the islands of Malaita and Guadalcanal in the southern Solomons, and the outlying Nauru and Ocean Island. The decision to take these last outposts was made to ensure that Japanese naval and air forces could cut the supply line between the United States and Australia and end any remaining threat from the south. Admiral Yamamoto organized a task force in April under the command of Vice Admiral Shigeyoshi Inoue consisting of four separate elements: a force to seize Port Moresby and southeast New Guinea, a second to capture the Solomon Islands, where air bases were to be established, a third covering force and a carrier group around *Shokaku* and *Zuikaku* designed to engage and destroy any American naval units sent to the area. The plan was to be completed between May 3 and 7.

Intelligence information warned Admiral Nimitz, who had recently taken over as commander of the Pacific Fleet, that a major Japanese force was moving south. He sent the U.S. carriers *Lexington* and *Yorktown*, both unscathed from the Pearl Harbor attack, to rendezvous with an assortment of smaller Allied ships to form a task force to oppose the Japanese. The Allied force, commanded by Rear Admiral Frank Fletcher, arrived in the Coral Sea, bordered by the Great Barrier Reef, just as the Japanese began their assault on Tulagi. On May 4 aircraft from the *Yorktown* attacked but failed to repel the Japanese landing. Poor weather and visibility made it difficult for the two sides to find each other. Fletcher mistook the light force converging on Port Moresby for the main Japanese carrier units and sent his aircraft to intercept. They pounded and sank the light carrier *Shoho* on May 7, after which the New Guinea task force turned back, anxious about the loss of air cover.

ABOVE The USS carrier *Yorktown* nears the Coral Sea, April 1942, photographed from a TBD-1 Torpedo plane that has just been launched from the carrier. A heavy cruiser, oiler and destroyer can be seen in the background.

RIGHT Vice-Adimral Frank Fletcher who commanded the task force for the Coral Sea battle. Nicknamed "Black Jack", he had a reputation for excessive caution and was posted to the North Pacific in October 1942, away from the main action of the campaign.

BELOW American navy torpedo aircraft attack the Japanese light carrier *Shoho* on May 7, 1942 during the Battle of the Coral Sea. The ship was the first Japanese carrier to be sunk and its loss forced the Japanese to abandon their attack on southern New Guinea.

FLEET ADMIRAL CHESTER NIMITZ (1885–1966)

Born of German-American parents, Nimitz joined the U.S. Navy in 1901 and rose to distinction in the interwar years as an expert on the new submarine arm. In 1938, he was promoted to vice admiral and the next year became Chief of the Bureau of Navigation. On December 17, 1941, he was chosen as commander-in-chief of the U.S. Pacific Fleet with the rank of admiral, and set out to reverse the disaster of Pearl Harbor. He was made overall commander-in-chief of Allied forces in the Pacific Ocean in March 1942 and was responsible as fleet commander for the Coral Sea and Midway victories. His "island-hopping" strategy led to the isolation and defeat of Japanese garrisons in the central Pacific for which he was rewarded with the title of Fleet Admiral in December 1944. After the war he became Chief of Naval Operations, retiring from active duty in December 1947.

ABOVE A Japanese torpedo-bomber takes off from the deck of a Japanese carrier. Although Japanese pilots were highly trained, during the Battle of Midway almost three-quarters of carrier pilots were killed or injured.

CAPTAIN JOSEPH ROCHEFORT (1898-1976)

Captain Rochefort was one of the leading American experts on cryptanalysis. He joined the U.S. navy in 1918, was trained in code-breaking and learned fluent Japanese. His wide intelligence experience led to his appointment early in 1941 to head the radio intercept office at Pearl Harbor. Here he assembled a large team of cryptanalysts and linguists who made it their task to break the Japanese naval code JN-25. During the early part of 1942 they succeeded in breaking the complicated cipher mechanism and could read some of the messages, although dates proved difficult. This intelligence information – known, like its European counterpart, as ULTRA – was vital for the Battle of Midway. The dating system was finally broken in May and Rochefort's unit provided the vital intelligence needed for the coming battle. From 1942 to 1946 he was in Washington as head of the Pacific Strategic Intelligence Group, and he retired in 1946.

remaining carriers after the Battle of the Coral Sea were far away to the south, protecting Australia.

This was the first of the Japanese miscalculations. Nimitz had two carriers, *Hornet* and *Enterprise*, and thanks to an extraordinary technical feat of repair, the damaged *Yorktown* was also available by May 31. The force was placed under the overall command of Admiral Fletcher, and the carriers placed under Rear Admiral Raymond Spruance. Against the Japanese four carriers, seven battleships, 12 cruisers and 44 destroyers, the Americans could muster only three carriers, eight cruisers and 15 destroyers. The one solid advantage enjoyed by the American side was intelligence, and without it the battle could not have been fought and won. The Fleet Radio Unit Pacific at Pearl Harbor could decode and decipher the Japanese main code, JN-25, and knew by May 21 that Operation "MI" meant Midway. A few days later, the exact time for the attack on Midway and the Aleutians was also known. The American strategy was to sail the small carrier force northeast of Midway, out of range of Japanese search aircraft and submarines. Once the Japanese units had been identified by aircraft from Midway, the plan was to assault them with waves of torpedo- and dive-bombers but at all costs to avoid the big fleet engagement sought by Yamamoto.

The battle represented a great risk for the American side, heavily outnumbered in ships and aircraft, but the failure of Japanese reconnaissance to detect Spruance's force until well after the attack on Midway had begun left the Japanese carriers exposed to a

dangerous counter-attack as their aircraft were refuelled and rearmed on deck. The American torpedo-bombers were too slow and the force was decimated, but around 50 Dauntless dive-bombers, undetected by the Japanese, dropped enough bombs onto the carriers' crowded decks to create havoc. By early next morning all four Japanese fleet carriers, *Hiryu*, *Kaga*, *Soryu* and Nagumo's flagship, *Akagi*, were sunk. Yamamoto ordered his battleships forward to destroy the enemy but in thick fog they could not be found, and without air cover the ships faced a great risk. *Yorktown* was damaged by aircraft, and sunk by a submarine three days later, but the great fleet engagement eluded the Japanese. The American victory was decisive, and it was achieved in a battle conducted and won by aircraft from two carrier forces that never even sighted each other. Senior Japanese commanders later admitted that this was the turning point in Japan's war effort. In 1943 and 1944, Japanese shipyards turned out another seven aircraft carriers, the United States built 90. The death and injury of 70 percent of Japan's highly trained naval pilots was never satisfactorily made good.

BELOW The Japanese cruiser *Mikuma* on fire after attack by aircraft from the USS carrier *Enterprise* on June 6, 1942. Despite continued American attacks, the cruiser was the only major casualty apart from the four Japanese carriers.

BELOW LEFT The U.S. carrier *Yorktown* was hit by Japanese torpedo-bombers in two attacks on June 4, 1942. Listing badly, the carrier eventually had to be abandoned.

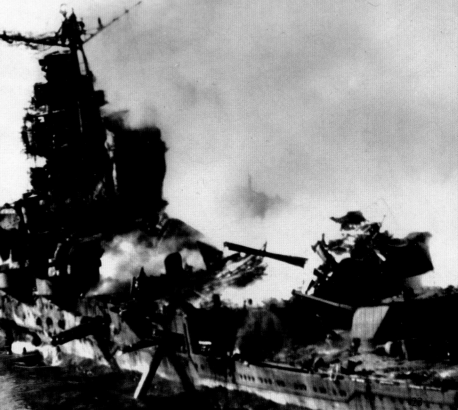

BATTLE FOR THE SOLOMONS

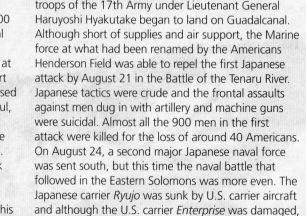

After the Battle of Midway the Japanese continued with their plan to interrupt communications between the United States and the South Pacific by taking over a string of island bases east of New Guinea. At the southern end of the Solomon Islands group, on Guadalcanal, they landed a small force to construct an airfield, while they planned to use the nearby island of Tulagi as a small southern naval base. Allied intelligence on Japanese moves encouraged the decision to launch a pre-emptive attack on Tulagi and Guadalcanal with the object of neutralizing the Japanese threat to supply lines and breaching the perimeter of the southern area of their advance. Vice Admiral Frank Fletcher commanded the U.S. naval force which arrived on August 7, transporting 19,000 men of the 1st Marine Division under Major General Alexander Vandegrift. The landings on Guadalcanal resulted in the rapid seizure of the Japanese airfield at Lunga, while after two days of hard fighting the port of Tulagi was captured. The Japanese command, based further to the north in the New Britain port of Rabaul, reacted at once and Guadalcanal, a small tropical island covered with inhospitable jungle, became, like Midway, a battle over the limit of Japanese advance.

On the night of August 8–9, a Japanese naval task force of seven cruisers arrived off Savo Island, in the strait between Lunga and Tulagi, where it sank four cruisers and damaged two more. Fletcher withdrew his

ABOVE A group of U.S. Marines landing in the Solomons during the assault on Guadalcanal leap from their boat and head for the shelter of the jungle rim. Beach assaults were the only way to gain a foothold in the long haul to drive the Japanese from their island fortresses.

TOP RIGHT Marine troops on Guadalcanal employ a 3-inch (75mm) howitzer artillery piece to bombard a Japanese position on the island.

carrier force, and over the next two weeks Japanese troops of the 17th Army under Lieutenant General Haruyoshi Hyakutake began to land on Guadalcanal. Although short of supplies and air support, the Marine force at what had been renamed by the Americans Henderson Field was able to repel the first Japanese attack by August 21 in the Battle of the Tenaru River. Japanese tactics were crude and the frontal assaults against men dug in with artillery and machine guns were suicidal. Almost all the 900 men in the first attack were killed for the loss of around 40 Americans. On August 24, a second major Japanese naval force was sent south, but this time the naval battle that followed in the Eastern Solomons was more even. The Japanese carrier *Ryujo* was sunk by U.S. carrier aircraft and although the U.S. carrier *Enterprise* was damaged,

ABOVE In the Battle of Santa Cruz off the southernmost Solomon Islands, a Japanese aircraft bombs a U.S. carrier. During the battle, the USS carrier *Hornet* was sunk along with a destroyer; the Japanese fleet suffered heavy losses of aircraft and damage to two battleships and two carriers.

BELOW Commander of U.S. carriers Admiral William F. Halsey was made commander-in-chief South Pacific Area in October 1942 at the height of the Guadalcanal campaign. He drove his men aggressively under the slogan "Kill Japs! Kill more Japs!".

GENERAL ALEXANDER VANDEGRIFT (1887–1973)

General Vandegrift joined the U.S. Marine Corps in 1909, and after service in the Caribbean, became a Marine Corps Assistant Chief-of-Staff, and by 1940, assistant to the U.S. Marine Corps Commandant with the rank of Brigadier General. Shortly before Pearl Harbor he was sent to command the 1st Marine Division, and in May 1942 took the division to the south Pacific where he led it in the first full-scale invasion of Japanese-held territory in the Solomons. The capture of the island of Guadalcanal earned him the Medal of Honor and promotion to command of a Marine Corps. On January 1, 1944, he was promoted to lieutenant general and became Commandant of the Marine Corps in Washington. In April 1945, he became the first Marine Corps officer to reach the rank of four-star general.

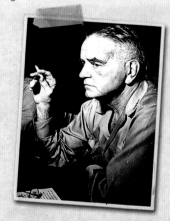

the Japanese force withdrew. Nevertheless, the build-up of Japanese forces continued under cover of night. They were used for further attacks on the Henderson Field enclave, but all of them were repulsed, including the battle for "Bloody Ridge" on September 12 when the Japanese troops were annihilated once again. By mid-October, both sides had approximately the same number of forces, 22,000 Japanese and 23,000 Americans, while the presence of large Japanese naval forces posed a serious threat to the American foothold on the island.

The week beginning October 23 was potentially decisive. The Japanese army began a series of heavy attacks on Henderson Field, and on October 25 a light naval force bombarded the area and sank a number of small vessels. A major fleet engagement on October 26 off the Santa Cruz Islands to the east of the Solomons led to the sinking of the U.S. carrier *Hornet*, but also to heavy losses of Japanese carrier aircraft. The multiple attacks on Henderson Field over the period October 23–26 were once again repulsed with heavy losses in a series of hard-fought engagements, in which the two Marine divisions were joined by U.S. army troops from the Americal Division. At the end of October, the situation was keenly balanced, but after three months of combat the U.S. garrison had only succeeded in securing a small section of coast not much larger than the area they had first occupied in August. Over the following weeks, the duel between Vandegrift and Hyakutake reached a bloody climax.

SERGEANT JOHN BASILONE (1916-1945)

Gunnery Sergeant John Basilone was the first enlisted U.S. Marine to win the Medal of Honor (right) during the Second World War, and the only enlisted man to win both that medal and the Navy Cross. One of 10 children from an Italian-American family in New York, he joined the army at 18, served in the Philippines, and after three years of service became a truck driver. He re-enlisted in the Marines in 1940 and won his medal on Guadalcanal for his heroism during a long engagement on October 24–25 against sustained Japanese attacks. He kept his heavy machine guns firing despite the loss of many of his men and helped to repel the Japanese assault. He returned to the United States but then asked to be sent back to action. He died in the assault on Iwo Jima on February 19 after single-handedly destroying a Japanese blockhouse and allowing his unit, the 27th Marine Regiment, to capture an airfield. He was killed by a mortar shell and his body later buried in Arlington National Cemetery. He was awarded the Navy Cross posthumously for his exceptional courage in action.

RIGHT Dead Japanese sailors in the campaign on Guadalcanal in the winter of 1942–3. Japanese forces lost 20,000 men in the unsuccessful attempt to hold on to the island.

BELOW An aerial view of Henderson airfield on Guadalcanal in the Solomons in August 1944, some two years after U.S. Marines assaulted the island and established a preliminary base there. The Lunga landing ground, renamed Henderson Field, was captured on August 8 and brought into operation by August 21.

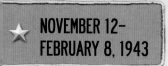
GUADALCANAL

ABOVE The Guadalcanal shoulder patch worn by those of the 1st Marine Division.

LEFT A Japanese ship in the major base at Rabaul is hit by a bomb from the U.S. 5th Army Air Force during an attack. Air attack on the base neutralized it as a threat throughout the conquest of the Solomons and the other southwest Pacific islands.

The battle for Guadalcanal reached a critical point by November 1942. Though on a scale very much smaller than the battles in the North African desert or around Stalingrad, the struggle for the island came to be regarded by both sides as a vital testing ground for American resolve on the one hand and Japan's capacity to protect her new-won empire on the other.

Japanese forces on the island were strengthened after the failures of the October assault on the American-held Henderson airfield by supplies and men shipped by Japanese naval vessels on the "Tokyo Express" supply route through the central Solomons. By November 12 the forces at the disposal of Lieutenant General Hyakutake exceeded American numbers for the first time – 23,000 against 22,000. But that same day a United States task force delivered reinforcements to Guadalcanal supported by air cover from aircraft carriers stationed in the Coral Sea and heavy bombers on the island of Espiritu Santo. By early December the balance was once again in American favour, 40,000 troops against 25,000.

This situation might well have been reversed had it not been for a series of destructive naval battles off the northern coast of Guadalcanal between November 12 and 15, in which a United States task force tried to prevent further reinforcement. A large convoy of Japanese troops, heavily supported by naval vessels, arrived off Guadalcanal in Ironbottom Sound on the night of November 12/13. A fierce ship-to-ship engagement followed which left six American ships sunk and cost the Japanese three, including a battleship. The following day American aircraft attacked the Japanese landing fleet, sinking a cruiser and seven transport ships. During the night of November 14/15 a second major naval engagement took place in which the Japanese battleship *Kirishima* and a destroyer were sunk for the loss of three U.S. destroyers.

REAR ADMIRAL RAIZO TANAKA (1892–1969)

A career officer in the Japanese Navy, Tanaka became an expert on torpedoes in the 1920s and taught at the navy's torpedo school. In September 1941 he was appointed commander Destroyer Squadron 2 and in October promoted to rear admiral. He fought in the invasion of the Philippines and the Dutch East Indies. During the Solomons campaign Tanaka's destroyer force supplied Japanese forces on Guadalcanal along the "Slot" between the islands of the Solomons group. The Japanese called the supply runs "rat transportation", but the Allies nicknamed them "the Tokyo Express". Tanaka became critical of Japanese strategy and was redeployed to shore duties in Burma, where he remained for the rest of the war.

RIGHT A tired U.S. soldier on his way back to Base Operations Camp on Guadalcanal, February 1943, after 21 days of continuous combat. The fighting conditions for both sides were exceptionally tough throughout the island campaign.

In the end only 2,000 troops could be landed with virtually no military supplies. The battles of Ironbottom Sound marked the end of Japanese efforts to save the position on Guadalcanal. One further attempt was made when Rear Admiral Tanaka personally commanded his destroyer squadron on November 30 in a run to Guadalcanal. His eight destroyers were surprised by a larger American force of five cruisers and four destroyers in Ironbottom Sound, but Tanaka's skilful handling of his ships produced a salvo of torpedoes that sank one cruiser and crippled the remaining three, before Tanaka retreated back up the Slot. The Battle of Tassafaronga, as it was known, was a tactical victory, but no supplies reached the embattled Japanese garrison.

In December 1942 the 1st Marine Division was replaced on the island by the 25th U.S. Infantry Division and Vandegrift was replaced as commander by Major General Alexander Patch, commander of the Americal Division. With more than 50,000 men under his command he began a series of offensives against the poorly supplied Japanese forces. By this stage the Japanese Navy command had already decided that Guadalcanal would have to be abandoned and the Japanese Imperial Headquarters confirmed this decision on December 31. The isolated Japanese forces fought with suicidal determination but were pressed back to the north of the island. Unknown to the Americans, Japanese destroyers off the coast successfully evacuated 10, 650 troops, including Hyakutake, between February 2 and 8, leaving Guadalcanal in American hands.

Japanese losses for the island struggle were high. Over 20,000 troops were lost, 860 aircraft and 15 warships. The United States Navy also lost heavily, but the ground troops suffered only 6,111 casualties, including 1,752 killed. This remarkable disparity in losses was to be repeated in the island battles across the Pacific. If the Battle of Midway had determined the limit of Japanese naval expansion, the failure at Guadalcanal decisively halted the onward march of the Japanese army.

ABOVE Two American soldiers of the U.S. 32nd Division fire into a dugout near the port of Buna in New Guinea in the drive to expel the Japanese from southern Papua at the same time as the operations on Guadalcanal.

BELOW Japanese prisoners, sick and hungry, are taken down to the beach by American troops after the capture of a Japanese stronghold on Guadalcanal, February 22, 1943. Most Japanese troops had been evacuated to safety by this time.

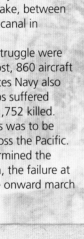

BATTLE FOR NEW GUINEA

While the struggle was continuing in Guadalcanal a second battle was taking place in eastern New Guinea where the Japanese had landed on July 22, 1942 to try to seize Port Moresby and expel Allied forces from the island. They landed at Gona and Buna and marched inland to seize Kokoda and by September were 25 miles from the port. Stiff Australian and American resistance and the crisis in Guadalcanal forced a Japanese retreat and on November 15 Kokoda was recaptured. On December 9 the Japanese lodgement at Gona was eliminated by the Australian army and on January 1, 1943 Buna was captured as well. Japanese failure in New Guinea was further evidence that the outer perimeter of the southern zone could not be made secure.

MONGOLIA

MANCHURIA

CHINA

KOREA

JAPAN

Tokyo

Nanking

Shanghai

OKINAWA

IWO JIMA

BURMA

Hong Kong

FORMOSA

MARIANA
ISLANDS

Rangoon

SIAM

FRENCH
INDO-
CHINA

PHILIPPINES

SAIPAN

GUAM

Admiral Yamamoto
shot down over
Bougainville Island
by U.S. fighter
aircraft after U.S.
intelligence
intercepts, April 18,
1943

Saigon

Manila

PALAU
ISLANDS

PELELIU

MALAY STATES

Singapore

BORNEO

CELEBES

Allied troops take Buna
after three months of heavy
fighting, January 22, 1943

Hollandia

Rabaul

NEW GUINEA

Batavia (Jakarta)

DUTCH EAST INDIES

Buna

TIMOR

Port Moresby

Darwin

INDIAN OCEAN

AUSTRALIA

PACIFIC THEATRE 1943

PACIFIC OCEAN

KEY TO MAPS

Imperial Japanese Navy		Australian military advances	
Japanese army		Air attacks	
Japanese military advances		Army land battles	
U.S. military forces		Airfields	
U.S. military advances		Limit of Japanese expansion	
Australian military forces			

MIDWAY

WAKE ISLAND

MARSHALL ISLANDS

Battle for Makin Atoll, November 20–23, 1943

SPRUANCE
Task Force 16

Battle for Tawara Atoll, November 20–23, 1943

GILBERT ISLANDS

SOLOMON ISLANDS

GUADALCANAL

BETiO, TAWARA ATOLL

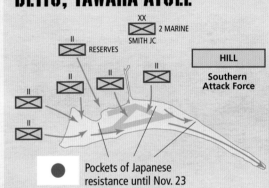

XX
2 MARINE
SMITH JC

II RESERVES

HILL
Southern Attack Force

● Pockets of Japanese resistance until Nov. 23

OPERATiON "CARTWHEEL"

Japanese reinforcements sent to Rabaul in April and November 1943, suffering large losses

EMIRAU IS.

ADMIRALTY ISLANDS
Feb. 29   Mar. 20

KAVIENG

NEW IRELAND

HALSEY
South Pacific Area

WEWAK
NEW GUINEA
BOGIA

Bismarck Sea

RABAUL

GREEN IS.
Feb. 15

SOLOMON ISLANDS

Australian-led forces capture Lae, September 15, 1943

MADANG
CAPE GLOUCESTER
Dec. 26
TALASEA
SAIDOR   Dec. 15
LAE
NEW BRITAIN
BOUGAINVILLE
Nov. 1   TOROKINA

SALAMAUA
ADACHI
18 Army
SHORTLANDS
CHOISEUL   Oct. 27–28

WAU
MOROBE
TREASURY IS.
Oct. 27
NEW GEORGIA
SANTA ISABEL

PAPUA

KOKODA   BUNA
Solomon Sea
Jun. 30–Aug. 27
RUSSELL IS.
MALAITA

PORT MORESBY
HENDERSON FIELD
GUADALCANAL

MACARTHUR
Southwest Pacific Area
ABAU   MILNE BAY

OPERATION "CARTWHEEL": WAR FOR NEW GUINEA

Following the defeat of the Japanese on Guadalcanal in February 1943, the Japanese naval and military leaders planned to strengthen their presence on New Guinea and to hold a defensive line from there through the northern Solomons to the Gilbert and Marshall islands. During the first three months of 1943, Lieutenant General Hatazo Adachi's 18th Army was transferred to the eastern coast of New Guinea and a large air component, the 4th Air Army, was based at Wewak, far enough from the American and Australian air forces in the southern tip of the island to avoid direct attack. The object was to move back down the island to capture Port Moresby, the target for Japanese ambitions a year before.

General MacArthur planned to consolidate the victory at Guadalcanal, which had demonstrated the growing superiority of American naval power in the southwest Pacific, by launching a major operation, codenamed "Cartwheel", against the main Japanese base at Rabaul on New Britain and the Japanese forces in northern New Guinea. On New Guinea itself an Australian army group, the New Guinea Force, with five Australian divisions and one American, was assigned to attack the Japanese based at Lae and Salamaua. The all-American Alamo Force, backed by a powerful naval and air component, was to neutralize Rabaul and attack New Britain and the Admiralty Islands, further to the north.

The Japanese attacked first in an attempt to seize the Allied airstrip at Wau but they were beaten off in bitter fighting. Then, on June 29, the Allied attack began on the Japanese bases at Lae and Salamaua. To speed up the advance, Lieutenant General Kenney's U.S. 5th Air Force built a secret airfield closer to the Japanese air base at Wewak from which he launched two devastating attacks on August 17 and 18, leaving the Japanese with just 38 serviceable aircraft. The Japanese army defended to the death, and not until September 16 did the Australians overrun Lae and Salamaua and another three months were needed before the whole of the Huon Peninsula was in Allied hands.

THE BATTLE OF THE BISMARCK SEA

On February 23, 1943, 7,000 men of the Japanese 51st Division embarked in eight transport vessels at the main Japanese base at Rabaul in the northern Solomon Islands, bound for northern New Guinea. They were escorted by eight destroyers. American forces had been warned in advance of the convoy through Pacific ULTRA intelligence and on March 2 began a series of attacks by day and night as the boats crossed the Bismarck Sea. All the transport vessels were sunk and four of the destroyers, with the loss of 3,664 of the division.
The Japanese commander in New Guinea, Lieutenant General Hatazo Adachi, was among the 950 survivors to reach the Japanese base at Lae.

ABOVE A Beaufort Bomber of No. 8 Squadron Royal Australian Air Force above the shoreline during a bombing attack on Wewak, the site of the largest Japanese airbase on mainland New Guinea.

While this first campaign was completed, U.S. forces landed on western New Britain on December 15. The previous month, strong carrier forces had neutralized any threat from the Japanese base at Rabaul, while the main concentration of the Japanese fleet, at the island of Truk in the Carolines group further north, was too weak to contest every avenue of American advance. After landings in the Admiralty Islands between February 29 and March 20, 1944, the American Fast Carrier Force commanded by Vice Admiral Marc Mitscher swung round to mount operations on the northern coast of New Guinea far behind Adachi's retreating 18th Army, cutting off his avenue of escape. Strong forces were landed at Hollandia on March 30 and Aitape on April 22. Adachi ordered his force to attack the U.S. perimeter in July 1944, but was beaten back.

BELOW United States troops rush ashore during the landing at Saidor on the northern coast of New Guinea, January 2, 1944. This was part of the coast-hopping operations designed to outflank the Japanese defenders during Operation "Cartwheel".

LEFT A Japanese national flag, given to Japanese soldiers by friends and family and carried to encourage personal good luck and patriotic virtue. They were inscribed with messages of good fortune and slogans of victory and honor to the emperor.

RIGHT An American unit on the Soputa front, near the New Guinea port of Buna, carrying wounded comrades back to headquarters after 11 days' continuous combat during the campaign to drive Japanese forces out of the southern areas of the island.

He retreated with what was left of his force into the high mountains inland, and played no further part in the war.

Operation "Cartwheel" confirmed that the balance of power had swung firmly in favour of the Allies in the southwest Pacific. Although the Japanese had held the long frontier of their conquered Pacific empire for two years, it was only because fighting in the tough tropical conditions of the region was a slow process, while Japanese forces resisted with almost complete disregard for their losses and in spite of debilitating diseases and persistent hunger. The refusal to give up lent the fighting a brutal character which Allied forces did not encounter in the Mediterranean or Western Europe.

BELOW INSET The Japanese commander on New Guinea, Lieutenant General Hatazo Adachi, arrives on September 13, 1945 at Cape Wom airbase, Wewak, for the formal surrender of his few remaining forces.

BELOW Australian soldiers crossing the Faria River in the Faria valley in New Guinea on their way back to base. Australian forces played a major part in the fight against the Japanese on the island.

31

ISLAND-HOPPING IN THE PACIFIC: GILBERT AND MARSHALL ISLANDS

LEFT United States Marines from the 2nd Marine Division wade through shallow water in the invasion of Makin Atoll. The U.S. commanders had little knowledge of Japanese strength on the island, but in this case the small garrison of 800 was overcome in three days of fighting which proved less costly than on neighbouring Tarawa.

BELOW An American cruiser fires at Japanese positions on Makin Atoll, November 20, 1943, during an operation in the Gilbert Islands, northeast of the Solomons.

The assault on New Guinea and Rabaul in the second half of 1943 was one wing of a two-pronged campaign. A second line of attack was launched through the Solomon Islands north of Guadalcanal and on into the Central Pacific against the outlying Gilbert and Marshall islands, viewed as stepping-stones to the distant Marianas, which were within striking distance of Japan for the U.S. Army Air Force's new generation of heavy long-range bombers, the B-29 Superfortress.

In June 1943, Admiral William Halsey's Third Fleet began the task of capturing the main islands of the southern Solomons. Rendova Island was taken on June 30, then New Georgia was attacked and the base at Munda

BELOW U.S. Thompson sub-machine gun, adopted by the U.S. Army in 1938 and used widely in the Pacific theater by all Allied troops.

THE BATTLE FOR TARAWA

The battle for the small island of Betio on the edge of Tarawa atoll in the Gilbert Islands was one of the toughest battles of the Pacific War. Only 4,500 Japanese Marines garrisoned the island, but they were well supplied and dug in to deep defensive positions, including 500 pillboxes and a network of concealed trenches. The U.S. naval force that mounted the operation included no fewer than 17 aircraft carriers, 12 battleships, and 35,000 U.S. Marines and soldiers. They attacked on November 20, 1943, but intense Japanese fire and difficult tidal waters pinned them on the beaches. There followed three days of fierce fighting, but vastly superior manpower and supplies gradually allowed the U.S. forces to gain the upper hand. At the end, only 17 Japanese soldiers were left alive, but a total of 990 U.S. Marines and 687 sailors lost their lives, a level of casualties that prompted strong criticism of the operation among the American public.

captured on August 4–5. Japanese convoys sent to help the endangered garrisons were destroyed in two battles in the Kula Gulf and the Vella Gulf, and on November 1, U.S. forces, supported by the 3rd New Zealand Division, landed on the main island of Bougainville, where air bases could be set up to bomb the Japanese base at Rabaul. Japanese reinforcements were hastily sent to the island, where the Japanese garrison numbered around 40,000 men, but Halsey was able to call on extensive air support to contain the Japanese threat while an assault by two of his carriers on the powerful fleet of Vice Admiral Kurita at Rabaul forced a Japanese withdrawal. The Japanese were bottled up on Bougainville until the end of the war, when 23,000 surrendered.

Further north, Admiral Nimitz prepared to assault the Gilbert and Marshall islands. A force of 200 ships was assembled, with 35,000 soldiers and Marines and 6,000 vehicles. On November 13, a sustained naval bombardment began against Makin and Tarawa atolls in the Gilbert Islands. The attack, codenamed Operation "Galvanic", began on November 20 against Makin atoll, which was secured by November 23 after limited but

PACIFIC THEATRE 1944

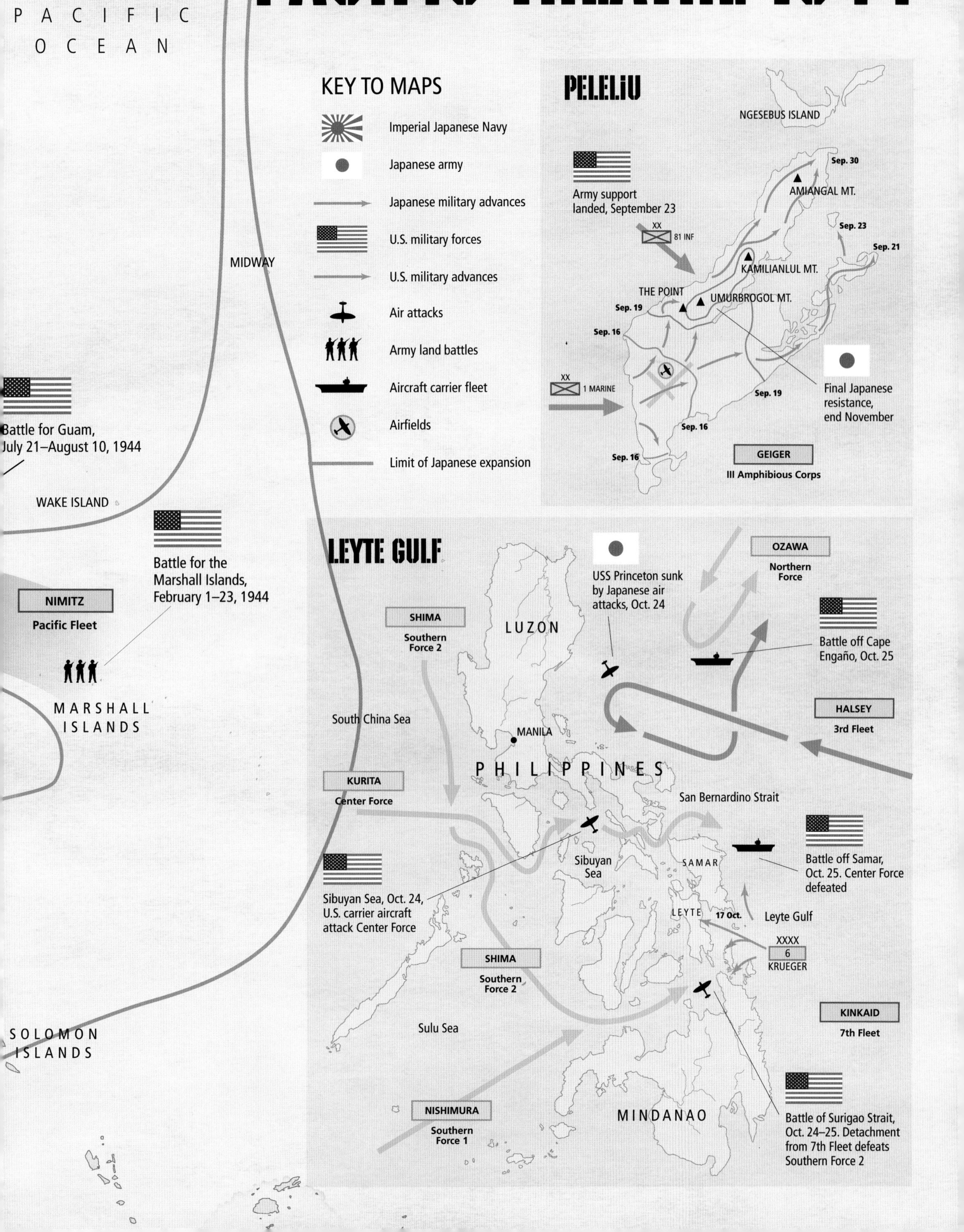

PACIFIC
OCEAN

MIDWAY

KEY TO MAPS

- Imperial Japanese Navy
- Japanese army
- → Japanese military advances
- U.S. military forces
- → U.S. military advances
- Air attacks
- Army land battles
- Aircraft carrier fleet
- Airfields
- Limit of Japanese expansion

PELELIU

NGESEBUS ISLAND

Army support
landed, September 23

XX 81 INF

Sep. 30

AMIANGAL MT.

Sep. 23

Sep. 21

KAMILIANLUL MT.

THE POINT   UMURBROGOL MT.

Sep. 19
Sep. 16

XX 1 MARINE

Sep. 19

Final Japanese
resistance,
end November

Sep. 16

Sep. 16

GEIGER

III Amphibious Corps

Battle for Guam,
July 21–August 10, 1944

WAKE ISLAND

Battle for the
Marshall Islands,
February 1–23, 1944

NIMITZ

Pacific Fleet

MARSHALL
ISLANDS

SOLOMON
ISLANDS

LEYTE GULF

SHIMA

Southern
Force 2

LUZON

South China Sea

MANILA

PHILIPPINES

KURITA

Center Force

Sibuyan Sea, Oct. 24,
U.S. carrier aircraft
attack Center Force

Sibuyan
Sea

USS Princeton sunk
by Japanese air
attacks, Oct. 24

OZAWA

Northern
Force

Battle off Cape
Engaño, Oct. 25

HALSEY

3rd Fleet

San Bernardino Strait

SAMAR

Battle off Samar,
Oct. 25. Center Force
defeated

LEYTE   17 Oct.   Leyte Gulf

XXXX
6
KRUEGER

SHIMA

Southern
Force 2

Sulu Sea

KINKAID

7th Fleet

NISHIMURA

Southern
Force 1

MINDANAO

Battle of Surigao Strait,
Oct. 24–25. Detachment
from 7th Fleet defeats
Southern Force 2

THE MARIANAS: DEFENCE TO THE DEATH

After the island-hopping attacks on the Gilbert and Marshall Islands in the Central Pacific, Admiral Nimitz, commander-in-chief Pacific Ocean Areas, determined to capture the Marianas, a group of islands including Saipan and Guam, which were within air radius of the Japanese home islands for attacks by the new Boeing B-29 heavy bomber. Air attacks began on the island defences in February 1944, and in early June, Vice Admiral Spruance's Fifth Fleet, with a grand total of 530 ships, arrived in the seas off Saipan to undertake a massive bombardment of Lieutenant General Yoshitsugu Saito's Japanese forces, whose estimated 25–30,000 soldiers were dug in to resist the American invasion to the last man.

On June 15, elements of Lieutenant General Holland Smith's V Amphibious Corps, the Second and Fourth Marine Divisions, attacked the southwestern beaches of Saipan through dangerous reefs and on beaches overlooked by high ground from which Japanese artillery could send a destructive barrage. Saito planned to contain the beachhead and then destroy it, but a steady flow of American reinforcements produced a breakout by day three and the seizure of Aslito airfield. Progress thereafter was slow against suicidal Japanese resistance and an operation planned for three days took three weeks to complete. On the night of July 6/7 the remains of the Japanese garrison in the north of the island undertook the largest *banzai* charge of the war. On July 9, when the overall U.S. commander Admiral Turner announced that Saipan was officially secured, Japanese soldiers and civilians leapt to their deaths from Marpi Point at the far northern tip of the island. The U.S. forces suffered 3,500 dead but only 2,000 from the 32,000 of Saito's force were taken prisoner.

Two weeks later, on July 21, Major General Roy Geiger's Third Amphibious Corps began the assault on Guam, an island ceded to the United States by Spain in 1898, which had been occupied by the Japanese navy at the start of the Pacific War. The island was defended by 5,500 navy troops under Captain Yutaka Sugimoto and 13,000 army soldiers commanded by Lieutenant General Takeshi Takashima.

They were dug in to prepared positions in the rugged mountainous district of the island around Mount Alifan. The beach landings on the west coast of Guam were less costly than on Saipan, though difficult to negotiate because of carefully constructed obstacles, but there followed a week of fierce fighting in which Japanese troops engaged in regular *banzai* charges, knowing full well that there was no prospect of reinforcement or fresh supplies. The island was finally secured by 10 August at the cost of a further 1,744 American dead. Only a handful of the Japanese garrison survived, retreating into the jungle areas where the last one surrendered in 1972.

While Guam was under attack, a further American assault was made on the smaller island of Tinian, three miles (five kilometers) south of Saipan, by 15,000 men of the 4th Marine Division. The island was secured by August 1, by which time American engineers (the famous

ABOVE An American battleship bombards the Japanese-held island of Guam on July 20, 1944, one day before the invasion. The bombardment by ships and aircraft was the heaviest and most co-ordinated of the Pacific War, leaving the Japanese garrison in a stunned state when the first wave of American marines reached the beaches.

ABOVE U.S. landing craft on the approach to the beaches on the west coast of Guam, July 21, 1944. The Third Marine Division and the Provisional Marine Brigade landed in two separate areas strongly supported by the ships and aircraft of Task Force 58. A destroyer can be seen in the distance.

ABOVE Japanese type 94 pistol. 70,000 of these were produced during 1935-45.

LIEUTENANT GENERAL HOLLAND "HOWLIN' MAD" SMITH (1882-1967)

Holland Smith is generally regarded as the father of United States amphibious warfare. He joined the marines in 1905 and saw service in the Philippines (where he won the nickname "Howlin' Mad") and later in the First World War in France in 1917–18. He remained a Marine officer after the war and by 1937 was in charge of operations and training at Marine Corps headquarters. In 1941, he became the first commander of the U.S. 1st Marine Division and in June that year was chosen to train the first dedicated amphibious warfare divisions. In August 1942, he took command of the Amphibious Corps, Pacific Fleet, which became the V Amphibious Corps for the operations against the Gilbert and Mariana islands. He commanded the expeditionary troops for the invasion of Iwo Jima before returning to the United States in July 1945 to take over the Marine Training and Replacement Camp. He retired in May 1946 and died after a long illness in 1967.

ABOVE During the invasion of Saipan the defending forces of the Japanese 31st Army dug in to well-prepared positions, using the rough landscape to best advantage. Here marines can be seen throwing grenades into a cave on a rocky outcrop on the coast of the island. Over 30,000 Japanese died in the defence of Saipan.

LIEUTENANT GENERAL YOSHITSUGU SAITO (1890–1944)

A career cavalryman who saw his first service as a very young soldier in the last stage of the Russo-Japanese war of 1904–5, Saito rose to the rank of major general in the Kwantung Army in China as chief of cavalry operations. In April 1944, he was appointed to command the Japanese Army's 43rd Division which was moving to Saipan. He became overall commander of the island's forces and organized the final *banzai* charge against the U.S. forces on July 7, determined that everyone should die rather than surrender an island so close to the Japanese homeland. On July 10, he committed hara-kiri and was given a final bullet by his adjutant.

LEFT A Japanese type 97 hand grenade. They were filled with TNT, with a time-delayed fuse of four or five seconds

BELOW A Japanese baby is carried down a mountainside on Saipan to a waiting ambulance jeep by a U.S. marine. The baby was the only survivor found in an area of Saipan where Japanese resistance was being cleared. Many Japanese civilians committed suicide rather than fall into American hands.

Construction Battalions or "See-Bees") had already begun to construct the first B-29 airfields. The battles for all three islands had been very costly to both sides, but Japanese resistance in defence of the outer perimeter of the home island area was now almost entirely suicidal. The fall of Saipan was greeted with dismay in Tokyo and the Japanese prime minister, General Hideki Tojo, was forced to resign from all his military and administrative positions, to be succeeded by Lieutenant General Kuniaki Koiso. The fierce defence of the Marianas made it clear that even if the defeat of Japan was now inevitable, the invasion of the heart of the Japanese Empire was likely to exact a heavy, perhaps insupportable, toll on the American forces involved.

BELOW U.S. marines and tanks advance against the Japanese 31st Army across one of the few level areas of Saipan. General Saito withdrew into the high mountains in the center of the island and three weeks were needed to finally dislodge him.

BATTLE OF THE PHILIPPINE SEA

Once it became clear that the United States was about to attack the Marianas, the Japanese navy launched Operation "A-Go", a further attempt to bring a large part of the U.S. Pacific Fleet to battle and at the same time prevent the fall of Saipan and Guam. Two large Japanese task forces, Vice Admiral Ozawa's 1st Mobile Fleet and Vice Admiral Matome Ugaki's Southern Force, were to rendezvous in the Philippine Sea before moving to engage the U.S. Task Force 58 commanded by Vice Admiral Marc Mitscher. Ozawa hoped that the prevailing trade winds would make it difficult for Mitscher's carrier aircraft to engage over long distances, while he could rely not only on his 473 aircraft and nine aircraft carriers, but also on shore-based aircraft in the Marianas.

On June 19, the stage was set for the largest carrier battle of the war. Ozawa had nine carriers, five battleships, 13 cruisers and 28 destroyers against Mitscher's 15 carriers and light carriers, seven battleships, 21 cruisers and 69 destroyers. The task for Admiral Spruance, in overall command of U.S. forces, was more difficult because it was also essential to protect the difficult invasion of Saipan, which had begun on June 15, but he had the advantage that intelligence sources had already identified the "A-Go" operation and reported the probable position of the Japanese fleets. Rather than seek combat, he and Mitscher waited for the Japanese to find them, confident that the much larger number of American aircraft, over 900 in total, would defend the fleet against attack. Even before the opening engagement, 17 out of 25 Japanese submarines were sunk, while land-based aircraft were destroyed on Saipan and Guam by heavy air attacks.

VICE ADMIRAL JISABURO OZAWA (1886–1966)

Jisaburo Ozawa was one of the Japanese navy's most experienced commanders and played a central part in the naval operations of the Pacific War. He was remarkably tall at 6 feet 7 inches (2 meters), and was later nicknamed "Gargoyle" by his men on account of his poor looks. He graduated as an officer cadet in 1909 and by 1919 commanded a destroyer. In the 1930s, he became a senior staff officer, serving as chief-of-staff of the Combined Fleet in 1937. Promoted to vice admiral in 1940, he became commander-in-chief of the Southern Expeditionary Fleet for the invasion of Malaya and the Dutch East Indies. In November 1942, he took over the 3rd Fleet and became commander of carrier forces and it was in this role that he suffered defeat in the Battle of the Philippine Sea. He tried to resign after the defeat but remained in post for the Battle of Leyte Gulf. On May 29, 1945, he became commander-in-chief of the Imperial Japanese Navy and, unlike many of his colleagues, did not commit suicide at the surrender, but survived to help with the demobilization of the navy.

RIGHT The war ensign of the Japanese navy.

BELOW A Curtiss Helldiver SB2C dive-bomber warms up on the deck of a carrier in Task Force 58, the carrier fleet assigned to support the island-hopping campaign in the Marianas in June 1944. Brought into service in 1943, the Helldiver had a radius of 895 miles (1,440 kilometers) and a top speed of 295 miles (475 kilometers) per hour.

LEFT The skyline is filled with anti-aircraft fire from the U.S. fleet under attack from Japanese torpedo bombers on June 19, 1944 during the Battle of the Philippine Sea. The picture was taken from the deck of the USS *Alabama*.

ABOVE The commander of Task Force 58, Vice Admiral Marc Mitscher, aboard his flagship, the aircraft carrier USS *Lexington*, on June 19, 1944, the first day of the battle which proved to be the largest carrier battle of the war.

When Ozawa's aircraft found Mitscher's fleet early in the morning of the June 19, the Japanese plan was already compromised.

What followed went down in American airpower history as the "Great Marianas Turkey Shoot". Superior U.S. aircraft, with radar and effective radio interception, destroyed the attackers at will. Japanese losses numbered 243 out of the 373 committed, while American losses were only 30. There then followed a further air battle over Guam which cost another 50 Japanese planes. During the battle, U.S. submarines sank Ozawa's flagship carrier *Taiho* and the carrier *Shokaku*, both of which were lost in the mid-afternoon. On the following day, Ozawa was unclear about the extent of his losses, but sailed away from the U.S. fleet hoping to re-engage. U.S. aircraft found his ships early in the evening of June 20 and, although at the end of their range and with risk that the aircraft would have to be recovered to the carriers at night, Mitscher ordered a wave of attacks. Another Japanese carrier was sunk and two badly damaged. Around 100 aircraft were lost during the battle, in the sea or in crashes on the carrier decks.

But Ozawa was left with only 35 serviceable aircraft out of the 473 with which he had begun the battle.

The battle was a major victory for the U.S. Pacific Fleet and it left the Japanese navy in a state from which it never effectively recovered. Ozawa was ordered on June 20 to disengage, having failed to sink a single American vessel or to prevent the final conquest of Saipan. His battered fleet retired to Okinawa, arriving on June 22. Mitscher ordered further attacks on Japanese shore-based aircraft, over 200 of which were destroyed during the course of the naval battle. The gap that opened up between U.S. and Japanese capability in the air spelt the end of any prospect that the heavy units of the Japanese fleet could engage and destroy the warships of the enemy. The Battle of the Philippine Sea, like the Battle of Midway in June 1942, was fought without a single engagement between surface vessels.

TOP RIGHT A photograph taken from the deck of *USS Birmingham* of a flight of 23 carrier-based fighters from U.S. Task Force 58 during the Battle of the Philippine Sea on June 20, 1944. The aircraft are preparing to intercept Japanese dive-bombers and torpedo-bombers attacking the U.S. fleet west of the island of Guam. In the "Great Marianas Turkey Shoot" the Japanese lost 65 percent of their air forces committed.

ABOVE A Grumman Avenger pilot, Roland "Rip" Gift, has a drink in the ready room of USS *Monterey* after a successful night landing on the carrier, June 20, 1944. Around 100 aircraft were lost trying to get back to the U.S. carriers at nightfall.

US SUBMARINE *ALBACORE*

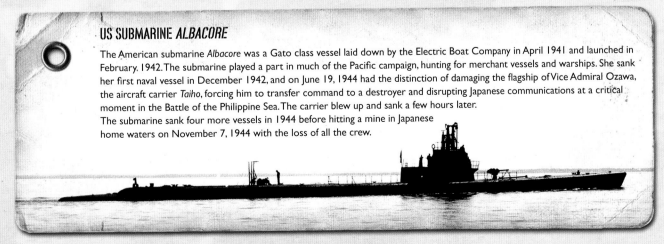

The American submarine *Albacore* was a Gato class vessel laid down by the Electric Boat Company in April 1941 and launched in February. 1942. The submarine played a part in much of the Pacific campaign, hunting for merchant vessels and warships. She sank her first naval vessel in December 1942, and on June 19, 1944 had the distinction of damaging the flagship of Vice Admiral Ozawa, the aircraft carrier *Taiho*, forcing him to transfer command to a destroyer and disrupting Japanese communications at a critical moment in the Battle of the Philippine Sea. The carrier blew up and sank a few hours later.
The submarine sank four more vessels in 1944 before hitting a mine in Japanese home waters on November 7, 1944 with the loss of all the crew.

THE BATTLE OF PELELIU

The capture of the small island of Peleliu in the autumn of 1944 was supposed to take only three or four days; the assault lasted two months and was one of the costliest battles of the entire Pacific War. The island was part of the Palau group, at the western end of the Caroline Islands. It had an airfield and the whole group of islands housed around 30,000 Japanese servicemen, 11,000 of them on Peleliu. The garrisoned island lay on the right flank of the planned army assault on the Philippines and its neutralization was felt to be an important objective by both the army and navy. When MacArthur won support from Roosevelt for the army campaign, the assault on Peleliu was finally approved.

The U.S. 1st Marine Division of approximately 17,500 men was detailed to carry out the assault. The commander, Major General William Rupertus, assumed that the island could be captured very quickly and adopted the conventional tactics of previous island campaigns. A heavy bombardment would be followed by waves of assault craft on three beaches on the island; the attacking force would then break the Japanese perimeter, capture the airfield and mop up remaining resistance. On Peleliu, however, the local Japanese commander of the 14th Infantry Division, Colonel Kunio Nakagawa, planned a different strategy to absorb the American attack. A battalion of defenders was left on the perimeter, dug deep into coral rock, with steel doors sealing the entrances to the bunkers and a mixture of heavy machine guns and artillery in support. The rest of his force was deployed inland, on the high ground of Umurbrogol mountain. Here, too, deep bunkers were constructed out of almost 500 small caves in the coral rock. Similarly sealed and provisioned with food and ammunition, the bunkers were designed to give a deadly field of supporting fire against any oncoming attacker.

RIGHT Hundreds of landing craft of the 1st U.S. Marine Division streak toward the beaches of Peleliu island during the initial invasion on September 15, 1944. Heavy naval bombardment from offshore vessels covers the island in a blanket of smoke.

RIGHT The Navy Cross, the highest decoration awarded by the U.S. Navy – a total of 69 were awarded to participants in the Battle for Peleliu.

ABOVE The 1st Marine Division storm ashore from beached "Alligator" vehicles at Peleliu Island, Palau on September 20, 1944. The smoke is from a burning "Alligator."

BELOW A Marine assault group advances on the beaches of Peleliu under heavy Japanese fire. The three-day air and naval bombardment of the island before the landing made very little dent in the Japanese defences.

MAJOR GENERAL WILLIAM RUPERTUS (1889–1945)

William Rupertus joined the U.S. Marines before the First World War and served in Haiti during the period of American belligerency in 1917-18. He was an excellent shot and the author of *The Rifleman's Creed*, a manual to encourage high standards of marksmanship. When war broke out against Japan he was an Assistant Division Commander of the 1st Marine Division. He played a part in the capture of Tulagi in the Guadalcanal campaign, and in 1943 assumed command of the division, which he led in the battle for Peleliu. In November 1944, with the island in U.S. hands, he was appointed Commandant of the Marine Corps School in Virginia, where he died of a heart attack a few months later.

Following a devastating air and naval bombardment, which began on September 12, 1944 and lasted for three days, the 1st Marines began the assault. Nakagawa's tactics worked with great success. The garrison suffered very little from the bombardment, and the shoreline battalion opened up a withering fire on the approaching landing craft. The Marines were pinned down on the beaches and took very high casualties. By the end of the first day little more than the 2 miles (3.2 kilometers) of beach on which they had landed were held. Casualties amounted to 1,100 dead and wounded.

The following day the 5th Marine Regiment captured the airfield and moved along the less defended eastern part of the island. By September 18 U.S. aircraft were able to use the airfield, and a week later Corsairs began dive-bombing attacks on Japanese dugouts with rockets and napalm.

The rest of the Marine force remained pinned down until the capture of the Japanese positions overlooking the landing beaches. Nicknamed "The Point", the rocky area was finally captured after bitter hand-to-hand fighting by the Marines of the 1st Marine Regiment, led by Captain George Hunt. At the end of the operation Hunt had only 18 men left in his company, with 157 casualties. The 1st Marines then moved on to the heavily defended Umurbrogol mountain where they found that Nakagawa had prepared a concealed and heavily armed mountain fortress. Over six days of fighting for what the Marines called "Bloody Nose Ridge", exceptional casualties were suffered. Japanese snipers picked off approaching Marines from positions high above them; at night small groups of Japanese soldiers infiltrated Marine lines and killed their attackers; unlike the usual *banzai* attacks, Nakagawa's men remained hidden and fired only when they could inflict losses on the enemy.

So high were Marine casualties – the 1st Marine Regiment suffered 60 percent losses – that on September 23 the overall commander of the III Amphibious Corps, General Roy Geiger, decided to bring in Army support. Between mid-September and mid-October the 5th and 7th Marine Regiments took 50 percent casualties along the mountain ridges. They were gradually replaced by the Army's 81st Infantry Division, which also took very high casualties. By the end of October the Marines had been withdrawn to rest on Guadalcanal. The Army continued to battle the ridge for another month before it was finally secured, though not entirely cleared. Each dugout had to be assaulted in turn with rocket fire, smoke grenades and rifle grenades. Like Japanese soldiers everywhere in the Pacific War, death was preferred to surrender. The Japanese death rate for the whole battle was 98 percent. Around 200 survived. The last Japanese to surrender on Peleliu gave themselves up in April 1947.

The island battle cost the U.S. forces 1,794 killed and 8,010 wounded, while Japanese deaths totalled 10,695. Although the airfield was brought into use, it proved unnecessary for MacArthur's assault on the Philippines or for U.S. naval operations further to the north at Okinawa and Iwo Jima. What the battle did show was the new form of Japanese battle tactics, which were repeated elsewhere. The closer the U.S. forces got to mainland Japan, the fiercer and more effective the opposition.

ABOVE LEFT A Marine on Peleliu. Casualties were extremely high – the capture of Peleliu resulted in 1,784 U.S. deaths and over 8,000 wounded.

ABOVE RIGHT Flames leap into Japanese caves from an amphibious tractor. The island was heavily fortified with bunkers and caves, and fire proved the most effective way of clearing the positions. Napalm was used here in large amounts. Mount Umbrigol alone had more than 500 caves linked by an intricate system of tunnels, making capture of the island extremely difficult.

ABOVE The M1919 Browning machine gun. It was used by U.S. troops throughout the Pacific War.

CAPTAIN EVERETT POPE (1919–2009)

During the horrific fighting to capture the high ground on the island of Peleliu in September 1944, Everett Pope led a company of the 1st Marine Division to capture what was called Hill 100. His bravery during the battle earned him a Medal of Honor. Pope was born in Massachusetts and joined the Marines in June 1941. He saw action in the landings on Guadalcanal in 1942 and the assault on New Britain in December 1943. His unit then took part in the campaign on Peleliu where, on September 20, his company of 90 men held off repeated Japanese attacks throughout the night. Low on ammunition, his men used coral rocks and ammunition cases to beat off the Japanese. When ordered to withdraw there were only nine men left fit for combat. He was posted back to the U.S. in November 1944. He finally left the Marines in 1951 and pursued a long career as a banker. He died in 2009 and was buried in Arlington National Cemetery.

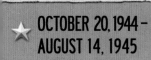
THE RECAPTURE OF THE PHILIPPINES

In July 1944, American commanders met in Hawaii to decide on the future course of the war against Japan. The navy favored a direct approach to the Japanese home islands, supported by air power, while the army, represented by General MacArthur, wanted to liberate the Philippines, first to establish secure bases for further operations, second as a point of honor to free the islands from Japanese rule. Roosevelt ruled in MacArthur's favor and in September 1944 carrier-borne aircraft began a systematic destruction of Japanese airpower on the islands.

The American planners chose the island of Leyte, in the more weakly defended central area of the islands, as the starting point for the invasion. In mid-October, 700 ships and approximately 174,000 men sailed into position. On October 17, U.S. Rangers landed on the smaller islands of Suluan and Dinagat to secure the approaches to Leyte Gulf. Three days later, on the morning of October 20, four divisions landed on Leyte against minimal resistance. While a major naval battle developed in and around the landing area on October 24 and 25, the Japanese 35th Army was pushed back and airfields were secured. The Japanese commander in the Philippines, General Tomoyuki Yamashita, the conqueror of Malaya, decided to make Leyte the point at which to contest the American campaign and 45–50,000 reinforcements were sent over the following two months. By mid-December, however, the Americans had landed some 200,000 men on the island, and organized Japanese resistance ended on December 19 with over 80,000 Japanese dead, although sporadic fighting continued for a further week.

While the grip on Leyte was consolidated, MacArthur ordered assault forces to seize the island of Mindoro

ABOVE Ships of U.S. Task Force 38 sail into Lingayen Gulf on the western coast of the Philippine island of Luzon shortly before the landings scheduled for January 9. Japanese positions were subjected to a heavy and continuous bombardment. The lead ship is the battleship USS *Pennsylvania*.

RIGHT American civilian prisoners of the Japanese at the Santo Tomas University prison camp in Manila welcome U.S. troops after liberation on February 6, 1945. Conditions at the camp, as in all Japanese camps, led to high levels of death from mistreatment and debilitation.

BELOW One of the most famous photographs of the Pacific War shows General Douglas MacArthur wading ashore at Leyte Gulf in the southern Philippines in mid-October 1944 to redeem the promise he made when he left in 1942 that "I shall return". The photograph was deliberately staged; MacArthur had come ashore less ostentatiously a little while before.

LEFT Badge of the U.S. 43rd Division.

RIGHT Badge of the U.S. 37th Division.

as a stepping stone to the conquest of the main island of Luzon. On December 15 Mindoro was invaded and by the middle of January 1945 it was secured. On January 9, two corps of Lieutenant General Krueger's Sixth Army landed at Lingayen Bay on the west coast of Luzon and rapidly advanced across the central plain to the capital, Manila. Yamashita decided not to contest the advance but to hold his sizeable army in the mountains, forcing the Americans to fight a protracted and costly campaign. Although the Japanese High Command had decided to abandon Luzon, and sent no further reinforcements from mid-January, the surviving garrison decided to fight to the death as had many others during the island campaign. Rear Admiral Sanji Iwabuchi retreated with a force of sailors into Manila and held out in the city between February 3, when the Sixth Army arrived, and March 3 when the Japanese force was all but annihilated. During the siege around 100,000 Filipinos were killed by artillery fire, conflagrations and the deliberate violence by the desperate Japanese forces. The

LIEUTENANT GENERAL WALTER KRUEGER (1881–1967)

Walter Krueger had the distinction of being born in Germany, the son of a Prussian aristocrat, and then after emigrating with his family to the United States in 1889, to have risen through the ranks of the U.S. Army from volunteer private to general. He first saw action in the Spanish–American war of 1898 in Cuba, then the next year went to the Philippines where he fought against the Filipino insurrection following America's overthrow of the Spanish colonial regime. He stayed in the army and was posted to France in 1918 despite French objections to his German origins. At the start of the Second World War, he was in command of the U.S. Third Army, but in January 1943 he was posted to the southwest Pacific in command of Sixth Army, in which he founded the Alamo Scouts, whose job, like the Chindits, was to act in small groups behind enemy lines. He led the army through all the campaigns of the region and ended up occupying Japan late in 1945. He was promoted to full general when he retired in July 1946.

LEFT The port of Manila under heavy artillery bombardment on February 23, 1945 as the U.S. Sixth Army fought for the capital. Caught in the crossfire are thought to have been around 100,000 Filipinos killed, many by the Japanese occupiers.

battle for Manila cost U.S. forces around 1,000 dead against 16,000 Japanese.

While Manila was secured, U.S. forces captured the Bataan Peninsula and the fortress of Corregidor, scene of the final American defence three years before. Before the fortress fell, Japanese forces ignited a large munitions dump, creating a colossal explosion, a fitting finale to the eclipse of Japanese power in the islands. Over the following months, some 38 separate landings to clear the southern and central islands were made by Lieutenant General Eichelberger's Eighth U.S. Army in collaboration with Filipino guerrillas. In June, Krueger's Sixth Army was withdrawn. Over the course of the whole campaign the Japanese garrisons, some of which continued to exist in mountains and jungles until the end of the war, endured overwhelmingly high losses. In the conquest of the islands the American forces lost 10,381 killed, 36,631 wounded and over 93,000 casualties from sickness and accident.

While American forces were securing the Philippines, a less glamorous campaign was waged further to the west, as Australian troops cleared Japanese positions in Borneo and the Dutch East Indies to secure the oil supplies there, while the remaining Japanese soldiers, beyond any prospect of reinforcement or assistance, spent the rest of the war in a vicious conflict with local anti-Japanese guerrillas organized by the Special Operations Australia units infiltrated onto the island in March and April 1945. The last Japanese surrendered only in October 1945.

ABOVE Troops of the 9th Australian Division land from a U.S. landing ship on the island of Labuan off the coast of the island of Borneo on June 10, 1945. Australian and Dutch forces, supported by Australian and U.S. ships, re-occupied key areas in the East Indies in the last months of the war.

RIGHT Japanese General Tomoyuki Yamashita, commander of Japanese forces on the island of Luzon, washes his hands after surrendering to the Americans on September 2, 1945. He was later tried for war crimes and executed.

THE BATTLE OF LEYTE GULF

The naval battle off the Philippine island of Leyte was the largest naval engagement of the war and it led to the final decisive defeat of the Japanese Combined Fleet. For once the balance of intelligence between the two sides tilted in favor of Japan. When Admiral Halsey's Third Fleet and Vice Admiral Thomas Kinkaid's Seventh Fleet arrived off the island of Leyte to launch the first landings, the Japanese naval High Command, under Admiral Soemu Toyoda, planned a final showdown with the American navy codenamed Operation "Sho-Go" ("Victory"). This time the American commanders did not know the nature of the Japanese plan and the final assault on the American invasion forces in the Philippines achieved a large measure of surprise.

Toyoda's plan was to lure Halsey's powerful Third Fleet into an engagement off the north of the Philippines with what remained of the Japanese carrier force while two other naval groups, Center Force under Vice Admiral Takeo Kurita and Southern Force commanded by Vice Admiral Kiyohide Shima, sailed through narrow straits on either side of Leyte to attack and destroy the American landings in a powerful pincer movement. The whole plan relied on Halsey taking the bait of an attack on the Japanese carriers, allowing the battleships and cruisers of the other two elements of the Japanese navy to overwhelm the forces left behind.

The battle plan worked better than might have been expected, since both the Southern Force and Center Force were detected and attacked when they

sailed into position on October 23. Center Force lost two cruisers on passage from Brunei, and a further battleship and destroyer to air attack in the Sibuyan Sea, west of Leyte, forcing Kurita to withdraw temporarily. The first branch of Southern Force arrived at the Surigao Strait, leading to the landing area, but was spotted by American motor torpedo boats and subjected first to torpedo attacks by destroyers, then, as it sailed in a straight line towards its destination, Rear Admiral Jesse Oldendorf's force of battleships and cruisers performed a classic crossing of the "T", subjecting the Japanese force to a thunderous broadside that sank all but two ships in the space of two hours. As the remaining ships retreated, the cruiser *Mogami* collided with a ship from the second part of Southern Force and was sunk by American aircraft during the morning of October 25. Shima withdrew from the battle, leaving Kurita to attack with only one arm of the pincer still intact.

On the afternoon of October 24, however, Halsey's

ABOVE The Battle of Leyte Gulf saw Japanese suicide attacks by aircraft for the first time. Here a Japanese Mitsubishi Zero-Sen "Zeke" fighter prepares to dive on the USS carrier *White Plains*. The U.S. Navy lost just six ships during the battle. Suicide tactics became significant only in 1945 in the approach to the Japanese home islands.

VICE ADMIRAL JESSE B. OLDENDORF (1887–1974)

Jesse "Oley" Oldendorf commanded the last victorious fleet engagement fought exclusively by surface vessels unsupported by aircraft when his task force defeated the Japanese Southern Force off Leyte in the Philippines. He joined the U.S. Navy in 1909 and commanded his first ship by 1922. In the early stages of the war he was posted to anti-submarine duty in the Caribbean and then commanded the Western Atlantic escort forces from May to December 1943. Posted to the Pacific in January 1944, Oldendorf commanded Cruiser Division 4 in the Marshall islands, the Marianas and the invasion of the Philippines. In December 1944, he was promoted to vice admiral and was wounded during the invasion of Okinawa. He commanded the Western Sea Frontier after the war and retired in 1948.

RIGHT The *Independence*-class carrier USS *Princeton* on fire during the Battle of Leyte Gulf following an attack by a land-based Japanese dive-bomber on the morning of October 24. Hosepipes are directed from the cruiser USS *Birmingham* in an attempt to bring the fire under control, but an explosion on the stricken ship badly damaged *Birmingham* before the carrier sank in the late afternoon.

VICE ADMIRAL SHOJI NISHIMURA (1889–1944)

Shoji Nishimura joined the Japanese navy in 1911, and became a navigation specialist, getting his first command, a destroyer, in 1926. In the 1930s, he was commander of the 26th Destroyer Group and entered the war as a rear admiral, commanding the 4th Destroyer Squadron. His squadron played an important role in the Battle of the Java Sea, which made him briefly famous in Japan. He then commanded the 7th Cruiser Division in the battle for Guadalcanal. He was appointed commander of the Southern Force for "Sho-Go", but his small force was annihilated and he was killed during the battle.

ABOVE A Japanese *Zuiho*-class carrier under attack on October 25, 1944 by aircraft of Air Group 20 from the carrier USS *Enterprise*. The photograph was taken from a torpedo-bomber a few seconds before the torpedo hit the carrier, which later sank.

RIGHT A line of American landing craft moves towards the beach on Leyte on October 20, 1944 as the U.S. Sixth Army, heavily protected by the U.S. Third Fleet, begins the invasion of the Philippines.

BELOW Troops from the U.S. Sixth Rangers battalion march to their embarkation point at Finschafen on the eastern coast of New Guinea before arriving at Dinagat Island in Leyte Gulf, which they attacked and captured on October 17.

aircraft had spotted the northern decoy force of carriers. Halsey ordered the bulk of his fleet, based around Task Force 38 (commanded by Vice Admiral Marc Mitscher) to steam north to engage. Kurita recovered his nerve and steered through the San Bernardino Strait with Center Force. There were only escort carrier groups available to protect the U.S. landings, with some 500 aircraft. They engaged Kurita's force when contact was made in the early morning of October 25, sinking two cruisers, while a third was severely damaged by a torpedo attack, but the superior firepower of the Japanese force sank two escort carriers and with the first use of "kamikaze" suicide planes, threatened to overwhelm the American covering force. But after three hours Kurita, uncertain perhaps of Kinkaid's true strength, withdrew.

By this time, frantic messages to Halsey had forced the Third Fleet to turn back towards Leyte. All four Japanese carriers had been sunk, but the miscalculation of Japanese intentions meant that the remnants of both Kurita's Center Force and the Northern Force were able to escape. Nevertheless, the separate actions proved a disaster for the Japanese navy, which lost 28 out of 64 warships committed and 10,500 sailors and pilots. The American naval forces lost six vessels out of the 218 sent to the Philippines. The superiority of American sea power, already proved in the island-hopping campaigns, now made the conquest of Japan's southern empire inevitable.

MONGOLIA

MANCHURIA

CHINA

KOREA

JAPAN

Japan surrenders,
September 2, 1945

Tokyo

Atomic bombs,
August 6–9, 1945

Firebombing of Tokyo,
March 9–10, 1945

Nanking

Shanghai

OKINAWA

Battle for Okinawa,
March 23–June 30, 1945

Battle for Iwo Jima,
February 19–
March 26, 1945

Hong Kong

FORMOSA

IWO JIMA

BURMA

Rangoon

SIAM

FRENCH
INDO-
CHINA

PHILIPPINES

SAIPAN

MARIANA
ISLANDS

GUAM

Manila

The recapture of the Philippines,
October 20, 1944–August 14, 1945

Saigon

PALAU
ISLANDS

MALAY STATES

Australian troops invade
Borneo, May 1, 1945

Singapore

BORNEO

Hollandia

Rabaul

CELEBES

NEW GUINEA

Batavia (Jakarta)

DUTCH EAST INDIES

GUADALCANAL

TIMOR

Port Moresby

Darwin

INDIAN OCEAN

AUSTRALIA

PACIFIC THEATRE 1945

PACIFIC
OCEAN

KEY TO MAPS

- ● Japanese army
- → Japanese military advances
- 🇺🇸 U.S. military forces
- → U.S. military advances
- 🇦🇺 Australian military forces
- ✈ Air attacks
- ✈ Bombing missions
- 🏃 Army land battles
- ✶ Airfields
- — Limit of Japanese expansion

MIDWAY

WAKE ISLAND

MARSHALL
ISLANDS

GILBERT
ISLANDS

SOLOMON
ISLANDS

IWO JIMA

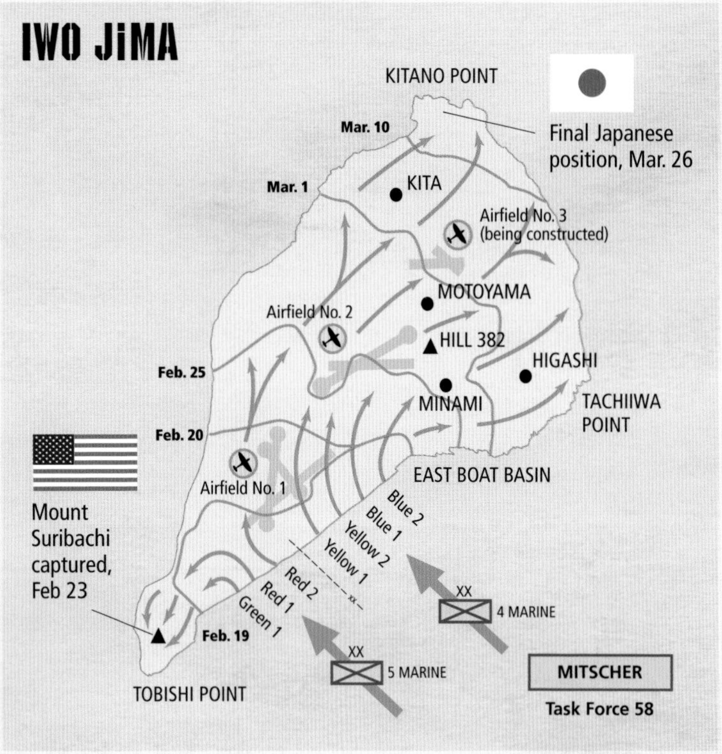

KITANO POINT

● Final Japanese position, Mar. 26

Mar. 10

Mar. 1

● KITA

Airfield No. 3 (being constructed)

Airfield No. 2

● MOTOYAMA

▲ HILL 382

● HIGASHI

Feb. 25

● MINAMI

TACHIIWA POINT

Feb. 20

EAST BOAT BASIN

🇺🇸 Mount Suribachi captured, Feb 23

Airfield No. 1

Blue 2
Blue 1
Yellow 2
Yellow 1
Red 2
Red 1
Green 1

XX 4 MARINE

XX 5 MARINE

MITSCHER
Task Force 58

▲ Feb. 19

TOBISHI POINT

OKINAWA

HEDO Apr. 13

● Kamikaze attacks against U.S. fleet

IE ISLAND

BISÉ
Apr. 12

XX 6

AHA
Apr. 19

TAKO

TAIRA

Apr. 8

XX 27

XX 77

MOTOBU PENINSULA

NAGO

TURNER
Task Force 51

ISHIKAWA
ISTHMUS

Apr. 4

● KIN

XX 6 MARINE

ISHIKAWA

Apr. 3

🇺🇸 End of Japanese resistance in north, Apr. 20

XX 1 MARINE

XX 7 MARINE

KUBA
Apr. 3

HEANNA

XX 96 MARINE

NAHA

Apr. 8

● Final Japanese position, Jun. 22

OROKU PENINSULA

SHURI
May 21

CHINEN PENINSULA

ITOMAN

Jun. 18

decoy move

XX 2 MARINE

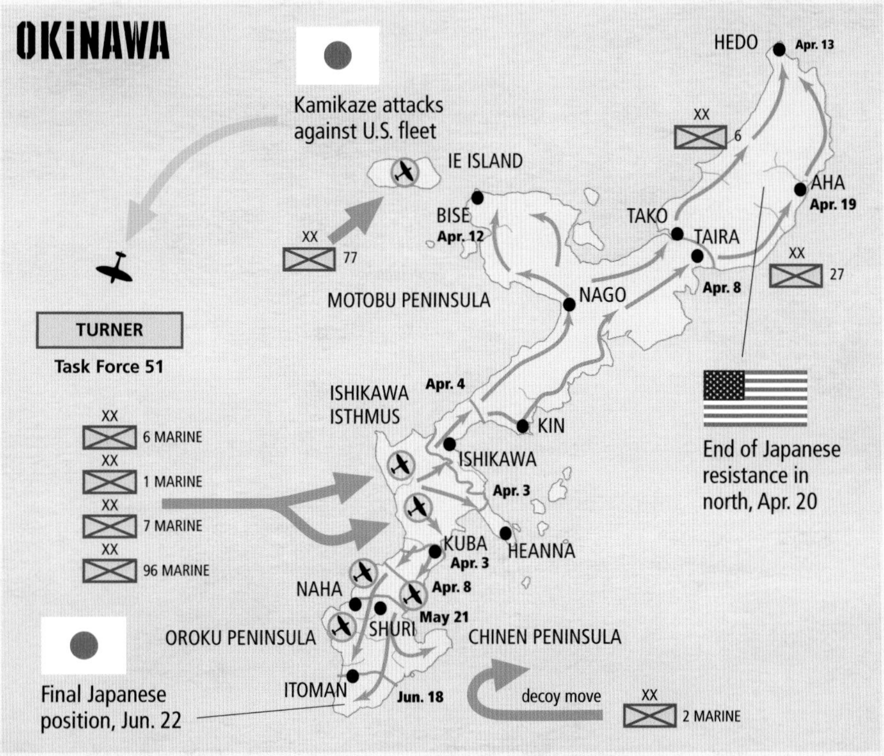

IWO JIMA

As American forces closed in on the Japanese home islands in 1944, a choice had to be made between invading Formosa (Taiwan) or other islands closer to Japan. The Formosa plan was finally abandoned in October in favor of attacks on the Bonin and Ryukyu Islands. On October 3, 1944, Admiral Nimitz was instructed to choose an island for attack which could be used by fighter aircraft to support the bombers flying from the Marianas. He chose Iwo Jima, a five-mile- (eight-kilometer-) long volcanic island 660 miles (1,060 kilometers) south of Tokyo where Japanese aircraft were based for attacks on American air bases in the Marianas.

The Japanese High Command guessed that the United States would try to find bases closer to the home islands. The local garrisons were strengthened and complex networks of tunnels and bunkers constructed. On Iwo Jima, Lieutenant General Tadamichi Kuribayashi commanded 22,000 troops dug in to well-prepared positions. The Japanese plan here, as elsewhere, was to allow the Americans to land and then to wear down their will to continue the fight in a brutal war of attrition.
The 72 continuous days of aerial bombardment prior to the invasion of the island seem to have done little to dent the fighting power of the hidden defenders.

The invasion force comprised the Fourth and Fifth Marine Divisions of Major General Harry Schmidt's Fifth Amphibious Corps, backed up by a reserve division, a total of 60,000 Marines. There were 800 warships eventually committed to the battle. The invasion had to be postponed because of the slow progress in capturing the Philippines, but on February 19,

supported by the first naval "rolling barrage" of the Pacific War, the Marines went ashore. The thick volcanic ash and steep shoreline made progress slow, and after 20 minutes the force was suddenly subjected to heavy flanking fire from hidden defences; some 519 Marines were killed on the first day. Nevertheless, the first Marines ashore succeeded in establishing a beachhead which soon housed almost 30,000 men. Most of Kuribayashi's force remained concealed in the defensive lines built further inland in deep bunkers and pillboxes carved into the soft volcanic rock. The first airstrip was captured on February 20 and Mount Suribachi four days later. By February 27, the other completed airstrips had been captured, but it took another month before the island was declared secure.

Japanese resistance so close to the home islands increased in intensity and the Marines took exceptionally heavy casualties. On Hill 382, nicknamed the "Meat Grinder", the Marines had to fight for every yard against defenders who fought until they were killed. Each defensive position in the gorges and caves of the rocky island had to be captured using flamethrowers and explosives to kill or flush out the

ABOVE The flamethrower was used extensively by U.S. Marines in the Pacific theater who realized its tactical value in helping to clear Japanese tunnel and bunker complexes.

BELOW Troops from the Fourth Marine Division land on "Blue" beach on Iwo Jima in the morning of February 19, 1945. They had to cross a high bank of soft black volcanic ash with full equipment. By the end of the day over 30,000 Marines were ashore and the beachhead secured.

LEFT Badge of a Japanese supierior private.

GENERAL HARRY SCHMIDT (1886–1968)

Harry Schmidt was Marine commander of the Fifth Amphibious Corps in the battle for Iwo Jima. He joined the Marine Corps in 1909 and had his first posting to Guam in the Pacific in 1911. After a long career on and off water he was head of the Paymaster Department of the Marine Corps when war broke out in 1941. In January 1942, he became assistant to the Marine Corps commander and in August 1943 commanding general of the Fourth Marine Division. His forces took part in the capture of Saipan and Tinian, by which time he was commander of the Fifth Amphibious Corps. His corps distinguished itself in the capture of Iwo Jima and went on to become part of the occupying force in Japan after the war was over. In February 1946, he took over the Marine Training Command and retired in 1948, when he was promoted to four-star general.

ABOVE Marines on Iwo Jima crouch behind a rock to avoid the blast from a heavy explosive charge laid in a cave connected to a three-tier Japanese block-house.

MOUNT SURIBACHI

One of the most famous images of the Second World War is the raising of the flag on top of Mount Suribachi, a small extinct volcano at the southern tip of Iwo Jima. The photograph was a staged replay of the first flag-raising by Company E of the 28th Marines on the morning of February 23, 1945, who seized the summit even though the mountain was still occupied by Japanese units. The first small flag was attached to a piece of waste pipe, but later that day a second patrol unit arrived at the peak with a larger flag and a war photographer, Joe Rosenthal. He photographed the men raising the second flag and created an iconic image.

ABOVE The U.S. Seventh Fighter Command base on Iwo Jima on the former Japanese Airfield No. 1 in the shadow of Mount Suribachi (right). Among the squadron of P-51 Mustangs is a Boeing B-29 heavy bomber, forced to land on Iwo Jima on the shuttle to and from bombing the Japanese mainland.

defenders. Even when forced into the open, many Japanese soldiers hurled themselves at the attackers rather than surrender. The sheer weight of American firepower from sea, air, and land drove the Japanese defenders back to the north of the island where they made their last stand in "Bloody Gorge" at Kitano Point which took ten days to clear and ended with a final suicidal *banzai* charge. Even though the island was declared secure on March 26, a further 2,409 Japanese soldiers were killed in the period up to June as defenders fought almost literally to the last man. The Japanese suffered a total of 23,300 killed, with nearly no prisoners taken. Marine losses totalled 5,931 dead and 17,372 wounded, over one-third of the original force committed.

Fighter aircraft began to operate from Iwo Jima even before it was secured and the first B-29 "Superfortress" bomber landed on the island on March 4, the first of 2,251 that made emergency landings on the island on the way to or from the Japanese home islands. At a high cost in lives, the air route to Japan was finally secured and the last stages of the heavy bombing of Japan's cities could be undertaken.

RIGHT Naval medical corps doctors and assistants at an emergency frontline dressing station. The poles have been stuck in the sand to support plasma bottles for blood transfusions. More than 17,000 marines were wounded, about one-third of the attacking force.

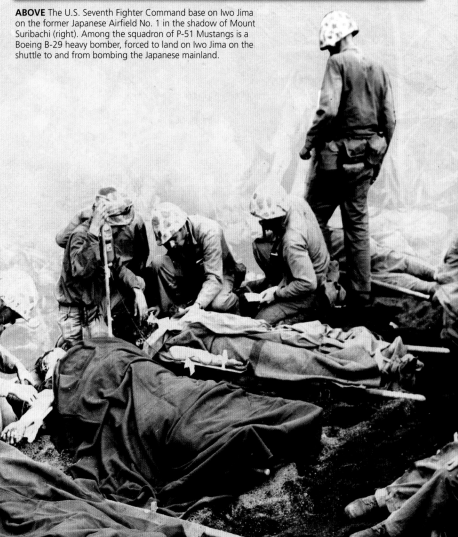

THE FIREBOMBING OF TOKYO

ABOVE Japanese children being evacuated from Ueno station in Tokyo. Around 8 million Japanese moved from threatened urban areas to the overcrowded countryside, placing a severe strain on an already overstretched rationing system.

LEFT Badge of Twentieth U.S. Army Airforce which included Twenty-first and Twentieth Bomber Command.

BOTTOM A Boeing B-29 heavy bomber at a base in China as it prepares to take off for a bombing mission over Japan. Most B-29 attacks were later made from the Mariana Islands in the central Pacific but from June 1944 attacks were made from China until the main airfields were overrun by Japanese armies later in the year. The B-29 had a range of 4,000 miles (6,500 kilometers) and could carry 12,000 pounds (5,500 kilograms) of bombs.

GENERAL HENRY "HAP" ARNOLD (1886–1950)

As chief-of-staff of the United States Army Air Force throughout the Second World War, Arnold played a central role in the American war effort. He became an army airman in the First World War, and by 1918 was assistant commander-in-chief of the Air Service, though he arrived too late in Europe to see combat. In September 1938, he was chosen to head the Army Air Corps with the rank of major general, and when the corps was turned into the Army Air Forces in June 1941, Arnold became its chief. He sat on both the American Joint Chiefs-of-Staff Committee and the Anglo-American Combined Chiefs Committee. In March 1942, his official title became commanding general of the U.S. Army Air Forces. He was an energetic, hardworking and sociable commander ("Hap" was short for "Happy"), with a clear understanding of technical development and high managerial skills. He suffered from poor health towards the end of the war, when he became the air force's first five-star general.

The bombing of Japan, like the bombing of Germany in Europe, began slowly and with mixed results. Because of the long distances involved, the bombers then in use in the European theatre were unable to reach mainland Japan from existing bases. Only when the first B-29 "Superfortress" bombers became available from the summer of 1944 – the first 130 arrived in India in May – was it possible to mount long-distance attacks against targets in the Japanese Empire in Manchuria, Korea or Thailand; the Japanese home islands were still difficult to reach for aircraft at the limit of their range. The capture of the Marianas was essential for the planned campaign of precision bombing against Japanese steel production and the aviation industry.

The first major B-29 raid was against the Thai capital of Bangkok on June 5, 1944. From then until early 1945, the Twentieth Air Force operated from bases in India and China against distant targets with very limited success. Operation "Matterhorn", as it was codenamed, achieved little and when the Japanese army overran the Chinese airfields the operation was wound up. Instead General Arnold, the USAAF chief-of-staff, decided to deploy the B-29s from the Marianas using Twenty-first Bomber Command under General Haywood Hansell, one of the planners of the air war in Europe. The first B-29 landed in October 1944 on Saipan, but a combination of slow delivery of aircraft, regular harassing attacks by Japanese aircraft, now using ramming techniques against enemy bombers, and the exceptionally long flights to mainland Japan in generally poor weather once again led to very limited achievements. In the first three months of operations, only 1,146 tons of bombs were dropped on a range of precision targets. The first raid on Tokyo took place on November 24, 1944 but the effects were slight.

The disappointing nature of the bombing campaign led Arnold

to sack Hansell and replace him with the more aggressive Major General Curtis LeMay, who arrived on Saipan in January 1945. After more weeks of unspectacular high-altitude precision attacks, LeMay was arguing with senior commanders for a radical change in tactics. He advocated using the newly available and highly effective M-69 firebomb in large quantities in low-level night-time attacks on Japan's urban areas. The subsequent fires would destroy local industry, demoralize the population and perhaps accelerate surrender. Uncertain whether Arnold would approve "area bombing", LeMay planned an experiment against Tokyo on the night of March 9/10. A total of 334 B-29s were launched from three island bases carrying over 1,600 tons of incendiaries and 279 reached their destination.

The aircraft arrived over Tokyo in the early hours of March 10, flying at between 4,000 and 9,200 feet (1,200 and 2,800 meters), where they met little resistance from the air defences. Pathfinders marked the area to be bombed with napalm, and the bombers released their loads indiscriminately within the designated zone.

BELOW U.S. carrier-based aircraft on a bombing raid against Tokyo on March 2, 1945. Aircraft from Task Force 58 and Task Force 38 bombarded Japanese cities and defences from March to August 1945 against light Japanese resistance. Aircraft also engaged in the heavy mining of Japanese coastal waters, bringing trade almost to a halt.

GENERAL CURTIS E. LEMAY (1906–1990)

Curtis LeMay masterminded the bombing of Japan and went on to play a central role in creating the U.S. Strategic Air Command after the war. He joined the U.S. Army Air Corps (later the Army Air Forces) in 1928 and had risen by October 1942 to the rank of colonel in charge of a bomber group of the Eighth Air Force based in England. A commander who flew with his men to experience combat, and a thoughtful tactician, LeMay was rapidly promoted. He was already a major general, the youngest in the army, when in August 1944 he took over command of Twentieth Bomber Command based in India for attacks from Chinese bases on Japanese targets in Manchuria and the home islands. He moved in January 1945 to take command of the Twenty-first Bomber Command on the Marianas and from here organized the bombing of Japan's cities. In July, he took command of Twentieth U.S. Army Air Force (which included Twenty-first and Twentieth Bomber Command) and later the same month became chief-of-staff to the newly formed Strategic Air Forces in the Pacific. After the war he became commander of the Strategic Air Command from 1949 to 1957, and in 1961 chief-of-staff of the U.S. Air Force.

BELOW An aerial view of central Tokyo following the firebombing of the city on the night of March 9/10, 1945. Only the concrete structures remain among the ruins of a highly flammable city where more than 100,000 lost their lives. The heat became so intense that people fleeing into the Sumida River (top) were boiled alive in the water.

The attack quickly provoked a firestorm which burned out 16 square miles (41 square kilometers) of the city and killed an estimated 100,000 people in a single night, the highest death toll of any single air attack. One million people were rendered homeless and a quarter of all residential buildings were destroyed. Over the next six months, LeMay's force destroyed 58 Japanese cities and inflicted an estimated 500,000 deaths. The new tactics of firebombing at low altitude proved grimly effective. An attack, for example, on the northern Honshu town of Aomori on the night of 28/29 July destroyed 88 percent of the built-up area. By this time there were 3,700 B-29s available, more than the Marianas could accommodate. There remains much argument over whether the urban attacks were responsible for reducing Japanese war production, since the loss of the merchant marine and attacks on communications played an important part in this, but there is no doubt that the bomb attacks quickly demoralized the home population and accelerated the efforts of those Japanese leaders who could see the war was lost to try to find some acceptable formula for surrender.

OKINAWA

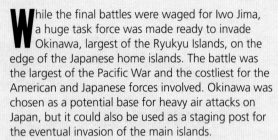

RIGHT Japanese open-faced flying hlemet

While the final battles were waged for Iwo Jima, a huge task force was made ready to invade Okinawa, largest of the Ryukyu Islands, on the edge of the Japanese home islands. The battle was the largest of the Pacific War and the costliest for the American and Japanese forces involved. Okinawa was chosen as a potential base for heavy air attacks on Japan, but it could also be used as a staging post for the eventual invasion of the main islands.

The preparations matched the scale of the "Overlord" landings in France the previous year. Under the overall command of Rear Admiral Raymond Spruance, Operation "Iceberg" eventually involved half-a-million men and 1,213 naval vessels. Lieutenant General Simon Buckner's recently activated U.S. Tenth Army, made up of two Marine and four regular army divisions, was given the task of clearing the island, but this time it was defended by approximately 100,000 Japanese troops, including 20,000 Okinawan militia, a much larger concentration than on Iwo Jima or Saipan. The invasion was supported by Vice Admiral Marc Mitscher's Task Force 58, which began a heavy naval bombardment of the island on March 23.

The Japanese commander, General Mitsuru Ushijima, decided, against the instructions of the High Command, to adopt the same tactics used on Iwo Jima, despite their evident failure. Most of the long, thin island was difficult to defend except for the limestone outcrops at the south end. Ushijima concentrated most of his forces in the hilly region of the south with a defensive line across the island from its chief town, Naha. Other forces were based on the Motobu Peninsula further up the west coast. The Japanese hoped to benefit from the decision, taken some months before, to use aircraft on kamikaze missions, employing the aircraft itself as a weapon to sink American shipping.

The campaign began with the seizure of the outlying Kerama and Keise islands between March 23 and 29. The main attack came on the morning of April 1 on the west coast of Okinawa. The invasion force faced little opposition and moved inland to seize the airfields. By the following day,

RIGHT U.S. Marines laden with equipment clamber down ladders into waiting landing craft on April 10, 1945 during the early stages of the three-month campaign on Okinawa. Over 170,000 U.S. servicemen saw action in the capture of the island.

BELOW RIGHT A concealed Japanese artillery piece on the island of Okinawa, part of the network of deep bunkers and shelters constructed in the mountainous southern tip of the island where the Japanese 32nd Army concentrated its forces.

BELOW The carrier USS *Bunker Hill* on fire after being hit by two Japanese suicide planes off Okinawa on May 11, 1945. The Japanese aircraft crashed onto the carrier's aircraft which were preparing to take off for an attack on Okinawa.

KAMIKAZE

In October 1944, the Japanese navy authorized the formation of a force of suicide pilots who would crash their aircraft deliberately into enemy ships in an effort to sink or disable them. The term chosen, *kamikaze* (divine wind), was a reference back to a medieval Chinese–Japanese war in which the Chinese fleet was dispersed by a fierce gale and Japan saved from invasion. The first official suicide attack was made on October 25, 1944 against the U.S. escort carrier *St Lo*. Large numbers were used in the Battle of Leyte Gulf and the peak of suicide attacks came during the invasion of Okinawa in April 1945. The aircraft were fighters or trainer aircraft, loaded with bombs; the pilots were volunteers initially, then supplemented by conscripts. They flew a total of 2,314 sorties and hit 322 Allied ships, sinking 34. The effect of the campaign was to destroy much of what was left of the Japanese air force for a very limited tactical gain.

"Ten-Go". From then until June 22, the fleet was subjected to 1,900 suicide attacks which caused high casualties among the crews, sank 38 naval vessels and damaged a further 368. The Japanese navy also launched a suicide mission when the giant battleship *Yamato*, together with a single cruiser and eight destroyers, set out to attack the U.S. fleet. The ship was sighted on April 7 in the East China Sea and sunk in an attack by 380 carrier aircraft, a dramatic end to what had been in 1941 one of the most powerful navies in the world.

Not until May 21 did the Japanese line begin to break. Naha was captured on May 27 and Ushijima retreated with his remaining forces to the Oroku Peninsula where a final ferocious encounter brought an end to Japanese resistance on June 22. Buckner was killed on June 18; Ushijima killed himself four days later. These were two of a high toll of casualties. Only 7,400, mainly Okinawan militia, survived from the 100,000-strong Japanese garrison, while total American deaths amounted to 12,520 with 36,631 wounded. The very high cost of securing a tiny island made the invasion of the home islands seem an increasingly hazardous and costly undertaking and played a part in the decision, taken a month later, to drop the atomic bomb.

the island was split in two as U.S. forces reached the east coast. The marine units moved northwards against weak resistance, reaching the north of the island by April 15. Only on the Mobotu Peninsula was there heavy fighting, but the Marine Sixth Division secured it by April 20.

The four army divisions faced a much more formidable obstacle when they reached the southern defensive line on April 9. The terrain favored the defenders and the American assault stalled. On May 4 in torrential rains that turned the ground to mud, the Japanese launched a powerful counter-attack which produced a prolonged hand-to-hand battle with high casualties on both sides.

From 6 April, the invasion fleet was also subject to repeated kamikaze attacks launched by the commander of the Japanese 1st Mobile Fleet under the codename

ABOVE A U.S. flame-thrower tank in action on June 21, 1945 in southern Okinawa towards the end of the campaign to seize the island. Flame-throwers were used to flush out hidden Japanese snipers. A U.S. infantryman crouches behind the tank to fire at Japanese soldiers escaping the flames.

BELOW LEFT An officer of the U.S. Tenth Army shares his rations with two Okinawan children found hiding in an abandoned tomb on the island. Thousands of civilians perished in the fighting or committed suicide.

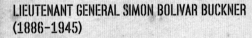

LIEUTENANT GENERAL SIMON BOLIVAR BUCKNER (1886–1945)

Lieutenant General Simon Buckner was the highest-ranking U.S. officer to be killed by enemy fire during the Second World War. The son of a Confederate general of the same name, Buckner joined the army in 1908, serving in the Philippines during the First World War. He was a tough trainer of men and was commandant of cadets at West Point in the early 1930s. He was sent to command the defence of Alaska in 1941 and was then promoted to brigadier general. In 1943, he seized back the two Aleutian Islands captured by the Japanese in 1942. In July 1944 he organized the U.S. Tenth Army for the conquest of Taiwan, but their destination was then changed to Okinawa and it was here, on June 18, 1945, towards the end of the campaign, that he was hit by shells from a Japanese battery and killed instantly.

LEFT
Marines of the Second Battalion, 29th Marines, Sixth Division flush out Japanese resisters on the Oruku Peninsula at the far southwest of the island on June 27, 1945, shortly before the island was declared secured. The Japanese soldier standing is holding a white flag, an unusual act among Japanese troops, most of whom fought to the death on the island.

THE ATOMIC BOMBS

The final defeat of Japan was long expected to be a costly and lengthy campaign and the determination with which the Japanese forces defended Iwo Jima and Okinawa reinforced this conviction. A campaign plan for what was called Operation "Olympic" was drawn up, but unofficial estimates suggested that there would be between 500,000 and one million American casualties in an invasion of the home islands, and although military chiefs thought this exaggerated, they knew that Japan would be defended with more than usual ferocity. The sea blockade and the bombing of Japan's cities would, it was hoped, produce the defeat of Japan without a full invasion.

It is against this background that the decision to use the atomic bomb was made. Since 1942, under the codename of the "Manhattan Project", a large team of scientists in the United States had worked to produce a useable bomb. The physics necessary to understand how a bomb might be developed and what its possible effects would be was pioneered in the 1930s, and by 1939 the theoretical feasibility of such a bomb was established. The problem lay with production. In 1940, a high-level committee of scientists in Britain, known as the Maud Committee, was set up to report on the bomb. In July 1941 the committee concluded that a bomb could be made in the probable period of the war from enriched uranium and in October Churchill's government gave the go-ahead. The British did not recommend using plutonium, a new element derived from uranium, but this was developed later in the United States and used for one of the bombs.

The economic effort of making the bomb proved beyond British capabilities, and in June 1942 the United States took over full responsibility for the whole project. British scientists moved to America and worked with a scientific team under Robert Oppenheimer. The

ROBERT OPPENHEIMER (1904–1967)

Robert Oppenheimer was the physicist who led the research on the atomic bomb as scientific director at the laboratory at Los Alamos. The son of a textile merchant, Oppenheimer was marked out from an early age as a scholar and intellectual of extraordinary power and range. He studied theoretical physics in Germany in the 1920s before returning to America as professor of physics at Berkeley, California. It was his pioneering work on nuclear research in the United States together with his charismatic personality and driving energy that made him a natural choice to run the scientific side of the Manhattan Project. His flirtation with American Communism did not prevent his work at the time, but after the war, as chairman of the General Advisory Committee of the Atomic Energy Commission, he made powerful enemies who disliked his radicalism. In 1954, his security status was revoked when he was investigated by Senator McCarthy's UnAmerican Activities Committee. He moved to Princeton as director of the Institute of Advanced Study and died of throat cancer in 1967.

ABOVE Glass bottle distorted by the effects of the atomic explosion, Hiroshima, August 6, 1945.

whole project cost $2 billion and employed 600,000 people, and by the summer of 1945 enough plutonium and bomb-grade uranium-235 had been produced to test and use atomic weapons. On July 16, 1945, at the Alamogordo air base in New Mexico, a plutonium bomb was detonated successfully. News of the explosion was sent to Roosevelt's successor President Truman, who was attending the inter-Allied conference at Potsdam. He approved the use of two bombs on Japanese cities. Whether this decision was taken principally to avoid an invasion of Japan, or to test the new technology or to impress the Soviet Union has been argued over ever since.

Some Japanese cities had not been bombed by LeMay's Twenty-first Bomber Command so the atomic weapons could be tried out on them. The first bomb was used against Hiroshima on the morning of August 6, 1945. Nicknamed "Little Boy", the 8,800-pound (4,000-kilogram) uranium bomb was carried in a B-29 bomber from Tinian. It caught Hiroshima's workforce on its way to work. Five square miles (thirteen square kilometers) were utterly destroyed and an estimated 120,000, about 40 percent of the city's population, died either immediately or within a few days from the effects of radiation. The second bomb,

LEFT The centre of the Japanese city of Hiroshima after the atomic bomb attack on August 6, 1945. The large building in the centre is the Industry Promotional Hall which was retained in its ruined state as a war memorial.

BELOW RIGHT An aerial view of the atomic attack on Hiroshima, August 6, 1945.

ABOVE A photograph of suburban Nagasaki in September 1945 after the second atomic bomb was dropped on August 9, 1945. This scene was five miles (eight kilometers) from the epicentre of the explosion.

ABOVE LEFT A Dutch medical officer examines two Javanese POWs who were caught in the atomic attacks on Japan. They were among tens of thousands of victims of the after-effects of radiation and blast.

ABOVE RIGHT Commemoration of the 60th anniversary of the dropping of the atomic bomb on Nagasaki by the B-29 bomber *Bock's Car*. Here shrine maidens attend the memorial ceremony on August 9, 2005 at the Atomic Bomb Hypocenter in Nagasaki.

carried from Tinian on the morning of August 9, was destined for the city of Kokura but it was obscured by cloud and the crew dropped the 10,100-pound (4,600-kilogram) plutonium bomb – dubbed "Fat Man" – on the secondary target, Nagasaki. The city was sheltered by hills and the blast effects less damaging, but an estimated 74,000 people were killed and 74,000 injured from a population of 270,000. Tens of thousands suffered the long-term after-effects of exposure to high levels of radiation.

The effect in Japan was one of disbelief at first, turning rapidly to terror at the prospect of further attacks. In reality, the United States was not yet in a position to drop a further atomic bomb, but the same day as the Nagasaki attack the Japanese prime minister asked Emperor Hirohito to decide on the issue of surrender. The effect on the Soviet Union of the atomic attacks was less startling than the Americans had hoped, since spies had already supplied extensive information on the Manhattan Project. Stalin ordered a high-speed programme of nuclear development and the Soviet Union detonated its first atomic test bomb in August 1949, by which time the United States had a further 298 bombs.

LIEUTENANT GENERAL LESLIE GROVES (1896–1970)

Leslie Groves is best remembered for two things. He was a senior military engineer who supervised the building of the Pentagon in Washington, and also military head of the Manhattan Project for constructing the atomic bomb. He joined the army in 1918 after education at the Massachusetts Institute of Technology, and became an officer in the U.S. Corps of Engineers. In 1940, promoted to lieutenant colonel, he joined the General Staff as chief of operations, Corps of Engineers, and deputy to the chief of construction. He was an energetic and ruthless administrator who played a major part in organizing the huge construction projects made necessary by the expansion of the U.S. military between 1940 and 1942. In September 1942, he was appointed as military director of the bomb project which he codenamed "Manhattan". He was one of the leading advocates of bombing the ancient Japanese capital of Kyoto, but was overruled. He retired in 1948 with the rank of lieutenant general, unhappy about the transfer of the nuclear programme to the civilian Atomic Energy Commission.

THE JAPANESE SURRENDER

The Allied demand for the unconditional surrender of Japan presented a more difficult process than was the case in Europe. Surrender was deeply dishonorable for the Japanese military, which was why so many Japanese soldiers and sailors fought literally until the last, or committed suicide. The military domination of decision-making in Japan and the prevailing ethos of sacrifice for the sake of the Emperor impeded any attempt by civilian leaders during 1945, faced with the inevitability of defeat, to find a formula that would satisfy both the Allies and the Japanese military.

The Japanese leadership also shared many illusions about the invincibility of Japan and the defensibility of the Empire. Only with the heavy destruction of Japanese cities in 1945 and the bombardment of the homeland by Allied ships and carrier aircraft was it evident to the wider population that the propaganda of victory had been a cruel deception. Yet in the face of defeat the military decided that the Japanese homeland would be defended at all costs under the slogan "The Glorious Death of One Hundred Million". In January 1945, a Homeland Operations Plan was formulated and in March a law passed to enforce the creation of People's Volunteer Units, followed in June by the creation of People's Volunteer Combat Corps. These people's militia were poorly armed and supplied, but the assumption among Japan's military was that death must always be preferable to dishonor.

In April 1945, a new prime minister, Admiral Kantoro Suzuki, was installed. While some efforts were made to see if there was an acceptable formula for an end to

EMPEROR HIROHITO (1901–1989)

Hirohito came to the throne of Japan in 1926, taking the name "Showa" (enlightened peace) as the designation of his reign. He was a reserved and scholarly man, with a lifelong interest in marine biology. His reign was at first characterized by a strong pro-Western stance and Hirohito endorsed the parliamentary system which in practice restricted his own extensive prerogatives as Japan's supreme sovereign. The political system allowed Hirohito very limited room for initiative and when the military came to dominate politics in the 1930s, Hirohito was usually asked to endorse policies already approved by the army and navy. He was personally opposed to the war with China and the declaration of war on the United States, but was presented in both cases with a *fait accompli* which he could not easily reverse. He was nevertheless unwilling for Japan to abandon its empire or to accept dishonor and as a result was a reluctant partner in the military imperialism of his cabinets. In 1945, he played a key part in finally forcing the military to accept surrender. He remained on the throne from 1945 until his death in 1989, helping to adapt Japan to modern democracy.

TOP LEFT The Japanese General Yoshijiro Umezu signs the instrument of unconditional surrender on behalf of the Japanese army aboard the battleship USS *Missouri* on September 2, 1945.

TOP RIGHT Admiral Lord Louis Mountbatten, supreme commander Southeast Asia Command, reads out the terms of unconditional surrender to Japanese military leaders at a ceremony in Singapore on September 12, 1945.

RIGHT Troops of the 25th Indian Division searching Japanese POWs in the Malayan capital Kuala Lumpur after they had been disarmed in September 1945.

hostilities, Suzuki continued to work with military plans for a final defence. On July 26, the Allies announced the Potsdam Declaration which re-affirmed the demand for unconditional surrender and committed the Allies to the democratic reconstruction of Japan. The stumbling block remained the question of the Emperor: unless the Allies would guarantee the survival of the monarchy, the government would not be able to endorse surrender. Hirohito had already let it be known through the Japanese ambassador in Moscow (Japan and the Soviet Union were not yet at war) that Japan wished to end the war, but his own position made it difficult to deliver what the Allies wanted.

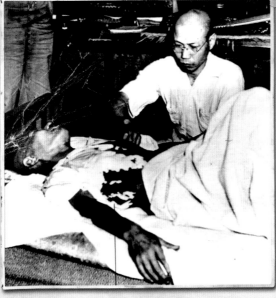

ABOVE A Japanese doctor attempts to staunch the blood from a self-inflicted wound sustained in a suicide attempt by the former prime minister General Hideki Tojo in Yokohama, September 1945. Tojo, who survived, was later tried and hanged as a war criminal in 1948.

The changed circumstances of early August forced the hand of the Japanese government. On August 6, the first atomic bomb was dropped and on August 8–9, before the bomb on Nagasaki, Soviet forces opened up a major offensive against the Japanese Kwantung Army in Manchuria. The Soviet army expected a hard fight in difficult terrain, but so weakened was Japanese capability that the million men, 5,000 tanks and 5,000 aircraft of the Far Eastern army groups overwhelmed Japanese opposition within six days, with the deaths of 80,000 Japanese. On August 9, Suzuki finally asked the Emperor to decide on surrender or a final fight to the death and the Emperor, who had already had secret intimations from the Americans that the throne would be protected, opted for surrender. He had to repeat his decision at an imperial conference on August 14, and the following day, despite continued opposition from the military, he made an unprecedented broadcast to his people that Japan would surrender.

The final process proved as messy as it had been in Europe. Some Japanese soldiers continued to fight on weeks after the decision to surrender. Many could not be reached in distant outposts and garrisons and the Allied troops had great difficulty in persuading them that the surrender was actually true. In Manchuria, formal surrender came only on August 21 and fighting continued in some areas until September. On September 2, aboard the battleship USS *Missouri* in Tokyo Bay, Japanese representatives met with General MacArthur to sign the formal instruments of surrender. Japanese forces surrendered in China on September 9, in Burma on September 13 and in Hong Kong on September 16. Japan was occupied by American and British Commonwealth forces; the Emperor was not deposed and played an important part in the democratic reconstruction of his country.

ABOVE Jubilant Manchurians greet the Soviet army as it enters Port Arthur on August 22, 1945 after a lightning victory over the occupying Japanese Kwantung Army. The Manchurian territory was ceded to China in 1946 and became part of the new Communist People's Republic in 1949.

BELOW The U.S. First Cavalry Division parading down a main street in Tokyo on July 4, 1946 during Independence Day celebrations. The commanders of the First Cavalry Division and the U.S. Eighth Army took the march-past in front of the Imperial Hotel.

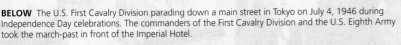

LEFT Badge of the U.S. 41st Division. This division was one of those to occupy the Japanese mainland following the end of the war in 1945.

MARSHAL KIRIL MERETSKOV (1897–1968)

Kiril Meretskov was not one of the stars of the Soviet military leadership, but he played a major part in the swift destruction of the Japanese army in Manchuria in 1945. He was also one of the few marshals not to have had military experience in the First World War. He joined the Bolshevik Party in May 1917, and was appointed chief-of-staff of a Red Guard unit despite his lack of any military experience. It was as a staff officer that he made his subsequent career, and he served briefly in the 1st Cavalry Army, of which Stalin was military commissar. His first major command was the war against Finland, where his troops failed again and again to break the Mannerheim Line. He nevertheless survived several bouts of Stalin's displeasure and for the whole of the European war commanded forces on the far-northern front against Finland and in defence of Leningrad. After forcing the Finns to sue for an armistice in September 1944, he was promoted to marshal. The following year he moved to the Far East for the brief war against Japan.

iNDEX

A

"A-Go", Operation 38–39,
Adachi, Hatazo 30–31, *31*
aerial warfare/bombing 12–13, 20–23, 30,
    32, 36, 38–39, 42, 50–51
Albacore 39, *39*
Aleutian Islands 22
Allied Forces 14, 20
Anglo-American collaboration 54
Anti-Comintern Pact 10, 11
Arnold, Henry "Hap" 50, *50*
Asian New Order 10–11
Atomic bombs 54–55
    Manhattan Project 54–55
    Maud Committee 54
Australia 15, 17, 20
    Darwin bombed 15, *15*
Australian forces 27, 30–31, 43

B

banzai charges 36, 49
Basilone, John 25, *25*
Bataan Death March 17
Battles
    Bismark Sea, Battle of the 30
    Coral Sea, Battle of 20–21, 26
    Leyte Gulf, Battle of 44–45
    Midway, Battle of 22–23
    New Guinea, Battle for 27
    Pelelieu, Battle of 40–41
    Philippine Sea Battle of the 38–39
    Solomon Islands, Battle for 24–25
    Tarawa, Battle for 32
    Tassafaronga, Battle of 27
Bismark Sea, Battle of 30
Blitzkrieg in Asia 14–15
"Bloody Nose Ridge" 41
bombers 13, 23, 26
    B-17 bombers 12, 16
    B-25 bombers 15
    B-29 bombers 36, 49, 50, *50*, 55
Borneo 15
Buckner, Simon Bolivar 52–53, *53*

C

"Cartwheel", Operation 30–31
Ceylon 15
Chiang Kaishek 10, *10*, 11
China, war with Japan 10–11

Chinese
    Communists 10
    Nationalists 10
Commonwealth forces 14
communism 10, 11
Coral Sea, Battle of 20–21, 26
Corregidor, Fall of the Philippines 16–17

D

Dutch East Indies 14, 15, 16

E

East Indies, Dutch 14, 15, 16
Executive Order 9066 13

F

"Fat Man" 55
February Incident 10
Filipino Army 16
Fletcher, Frank (Black Jack) 20–21, *20*, 23,
    24
French, Vichy 11

G

Geiger, Roy 36, 41
Germany, Tripartite Pact 11
Gilbert Islands 32–33
"Great Marianas Turkey Shoot" 39
Groves, Leslie 55, 55
Guadalcanal 24–27

H

Halsey, William 22, *24*, 32, 42
Hansell, Haywood 50
Hart, Thomas 17
Hawaii, Pearl Harbor 12–13
Henderson Field 24, 25, 26
Hirohito, Emperor Showa 10, 55, 56, *56*
Hiroshima 55,
Hitler, Adolf *11*, 55
Homma, Masaharu 16–17, *16*
Hong Kong 14, *15*
Hunt, George 41
Hyakutake, Haruyoshi 24–27

i

"Iceberg" 52–53
Imperial Japan 10–11
Imperial Rule Assistance Association 10
Inoue, Shigeyoshi 20
intelligence 23, 24, 38
island-hopping campaigns 20, 30–33
Italy, Tripartite Pact 11
Iwo Jima 48–49

J

Japan
    Hiroshima 55,
    Imperial Japan 10–11
    Imperial Rule Assistance Association 10
    Nagasaki 55,
    Okinawa 52–53
    Pearl Harbor 12–13
    start of war with United States 11
    surrender 56–57
    Tripartite Pact 11
    Tokyo, firebombing of 50–51
    war with China 10
Japanese Americans 13
Japanese Army
    Kwantung Army 10
    in China 10
jungle warfare 14

K

kamikazi missions 45, 52
Kimmel, Husband E. 12
King, Edward 17
Kinkaid, Thomas 42
Krueger, Walter 43, *43*
Kurita, Takeo 44–45
    Kurubachi, Tadamichi 48–49
Kwantung (Japanese army) 10

L

League of Nations 10
Lemay, Curtis 51, *51*
Leyte Gulf, Battle of 44–45
"Little Boy" 55

M

MacArthur, Douglas 14, *14*, 16–17, 30, 33, 40, 42–43, *42*, 57
Malaya 14, 16
Manchuria 10, 17, 57
Manhattan Project 54–55
Mao Zedong *10*
Marianas 32–33, 36–37, 38–39, 48, 50
Marshall Islands 12, 32–33
Meretskov, Kiril 57, *57*
"MI", Operation 22–23
Midway, Battle of 22–23
Mitscher, Marc A 30, 33, *33*, 38–39, *39*, 45, 52
Mongolia 11
Mount Suribachi 49, *49*

N

Nagasaki 55
Nagumo, Chuichi 12, 13, 15, *15*, 22
Nakagawa, Kunio 40–41
Nanking 10, 11
napalm 41, 51
Nationalists, Chinese 10
naval warfare 20–23, 32–33, 36, 38–39, 42, 44–45, 52–53
New Guinea, 21, 30–31, 32
    Battle for New Guinea 27
New Order, Asian 10–11
New Zealand forces 32
Nimitz, Chester 20, *20*, 23, 32, 33, 36, 48
Nishimura, Shoji 45, *45*
jungle warfare 14

O

Okinawa 52–53
Oldendorf, Jesse B (Oley) 44, *44*, 45
Operations
    "A-Go" 38
    "Cartwheel" 30–31
    "Iceberg" 52–53
    "MI" 22–23
Oppenheimer, Robert 54, *54*
Ozawa, Jisaburo 38–39, *38*

P

Pacific Fleet, U.S. 21, 22
Pacific, Western Area 22
Pact, Tripartite 11
Patch, Alexander 27
Pearl Harbor 12–13, 20
Pelelieu, Battle of 40–41
Philippines 12, 15
    fall of 16–17
    Leyte Gulf, Battle of 44–45
    Philippine Sea, Battle of the 38–39
    recapture of 42–43
Pope, Everett 41, *41*
Potsdam Conference 54, 56
POWs *15*, 17, *42*

Q

Quezon, Manuel *16*

R

Rape of Nanking 10
Rabaul 24, 26, 31, 32–33
Rochefort, Joseph 23, *23*
Roosevelt, Franklin D. 11, *12*, 43
Rupertus, William 40, *40*

S

Saito, Yoshitsugu 36–37, *37*
Schmidt, Harry 48–49, *48*
Shima, Kiyohide 44–45
Short, Walter 12
Shri Lanka, see Ceylon
Singapore 14
Sino-Japanese conflict 10
Smith, Holland "Howlin' Mad" 36, *36*
Solomon Islands 15, 21, 30–31
    Battle for 24–25
Soviet forces against Japan 10, 11
Spruance, Raymond 22–23, *22*, 36, 52
Stalin, Josef 55
submarines 13, 22, 39
Sugimoto, Yutaka 36
Suribachi, Mount 49, *49*
surrender
    Filipino 16–17
    Japanese 56–57
Suzuki, Kantoro 56, 57

T

Takagi, Tageo 21
Takahashi, Ibo 15
Takashima, Takeshi 36
Tanake, Raizo 26–27, *26*
Tarawa, Battle for 32
Tassafaronga, Battle of 27
Thailand 14
"Tokyo Express" supply route 26
Tokyo, firebombing of 50–51
Tojo, Hideki 12, *12*
Toyoda, Soemu 42
Tripartite Pact 11
Truman, Harry S 54

U

Ugaki, Matome 38
ULTRA 23
United States
    start of aggression between U.S. and Japan 11
    forces 16–17, 20–27, 30–31, 38–39, 42–43, 48–49
    Pearl Harbor 12–13
Ushijima, Mitsuru 52–53

V

Vandergrift, Alexander 24, *24*

W

Wainwright, Jonathan 17, *17*

Y

Yamashita, Tomoyuki 14, 42, *43*
Yamamoto, Isoroku 20–21, *21*, 22, 23

Z

Zhou Enlai *10*

CREDITS

The publisher would like the thank the following people for their valuable assistance with the preparation of this book:

Julia Dye, Warriors Inc
Jim Zobel, MacArthur Memorial
Dave and Eric, Wartime Press
Gina McNeely

PHOTOGRAPHS

The publishers would like to thank the following sources for their kind permission to reproduce the pictures in the book:

Key: t = top, b = bottom, l = left, r = right and c = centre

Akg-Images: 54tr, 57tr, 57br

Australian War Memorial: 30tc (042999), 30bl (127965), 30bl (REL34921), 30br (016422), 31tr (P00554.002), 31cr (070242), 31br (042740)

Corbis: 15tr, 15cr, 32cl, 33br, 39cr, 40br, 41tc, 41tr, 55br; /Bettmann: 10cr, 10bc, 11br, 13tr, 15tc, 32cr, 33c, 57bl; /Hulton-Deutsch Collection: 11bl; /Peace Memorial Museum/Epa: 54cr

Getty Images: 10tc, 10br, 12tr, 14tc, 27c, 27br, 33tl, 33cl, 33bl, 50tc, 50cr, 50bc, 51tr, 55tr, 55c, 55cr, 57tc

Imperial War Museum: 11tr (HU 75995). 13cl (NYP 68079), 13bl (EN 21474), 14c (INS 7204), 14bl (NYP 45042), 15tl (HU 2779), 15br (NY 7343), 32cr (NYF 11281), 37cl (MUN 3433), 38cr (FLA 5500), 45cl (NYF 57021), 52bl (HU 51237), 53tc (EQU 4088), 54bl (EPH 4631), 54b (MH 29427), 55tl (HU 044878), 56tc (A 30427 A), 56tr (A 30492), 56bc (HU 53442), 56br (IND 4848)

National Archives, Washington D.C.: 5, 7, 12tc, 12bc, 13tl, 13cr, 16tr, 16tc, 16cr, 16bc, 16bl, 17tl, 17bl, 17tc, 17br, 20tc, 20tr, 20bc, 20br, 21tl, 21cl, 21cr, 21br, 22tc, 22cr, 22br, 22cl, 23tc, 23cr, 23bl, 23br, 24tr, 24cl, 24cr, 24bl, 24br, 25tl, 25cr,

25br, 36tr, 36bl, 36br, 37tl, 37bl, 37br, 39tl, 39tr, 39br, 42tr, 42bl, 42br, 43tl, 43tc, 43bl, 43cr, 43br, 44tr, 44bl, 44br, 45tl, 45tr, 45br, 48tc, 48bl, 48br, 49tl, 49tr, 49bl, 49br, 52tr, 52c, 52br, 53tl, 53cr, 53bl, 53br, 58, 59, 60

Press Association Images/AP Photo: 26tc, 26br, 27tc, 27bl, 40tr, 40br

Private Collection: 25tc, 26bc, 37tr

Topfoto.co.uk: 14cr, 31tc; /Ullstein Bild: 14br

United States Marine Corps: 40cl, 41c

U.S. Navy Historical Society: 23tr

All other images photographed with kind permission of the Imperial War Museum and Private Collections.

Every effort has been made to acknowledge correctly and contact the source and/or copyright holder of each picture, and Carlton Books apologizes for any unintentional errors or omissions, which will be corrected in future editions of this book.

MEMORABILIA

The publishers would like to thank the **National Archives, Washington, US** for their kind permission to reproduce the memorabilia items in this book.

Every effort has been made to acknowledge correctly and contact the source and/or copyright holder of each item of memorabilia, and Carlton Books apologizes for any unintentional errors or omissions, which will be corrected in future editions of this book.

FURTHER INFORMATION

The National Archives of the United States of America: www.archives.gov

The MacArthur Memorial, Norfolk, VA: www.macarthurmemorial.org

Wartime Press: wartimepress.com

Warriors Inc: http://warriorsinc.com/

PUBLISHING CREDITS

Editorial Director: Piers Murray Hill
Executive Editor: Gemma Maclagan
Additional Editorial work: Alice Payne
Design Director: Russell Porter
Design: Russell Porter, Advantage London and Rachel Burgess
Cartography: Martin Brown and Russell Porter
Picture Research: Steve Behan
Production: Rachel Burgess
Cover Design: Russell Porter and Russell Knowles